ABC RADIO'S

Q&A

COOK
BOOK

ABC RADIO'S

Q&A

COOK
BOOK

PETER McCORMACK

Published by ABC Enterprises
and William Collins Pty Ltd, Sydney for the
AUSTRALIAN BROADCASTING CORPORATION
145 Elizabeth Street Sydney NSW
Box 9994 GPO Sydney NSW 2001

William Collins Pty Ltd
55 Clarence Street Sydney 2000

National Library of Australia
Cataloguing-in-Publication entry
ABC radio's Q & A cookbook.
Includes index.
ISBN 0 642 52709 1.
1. Cookery. I. McCormack, Peter, 1932- .II.
Australian Broadcasting Corporation.
641.5

Designed by Maree Cunnington
Edited by Nina Riemer
Illustrated by Bruce Goold
Photographed by Rodney Weidland. Art Direction by
Maree Cunnington. Props by Appley Hoare.
Food by Katie Webb.
Set in 12/13pt Plantin by Love Computer Typesetting,
Sydney
Printed and bound in Australia by Globe Press,
Melbourne

109894-10-995

Front Cover: Celery Soup, Treacle and Malt Bread
Back Cover: Vanochka, Swiss Chocolate Cake, Welsh Cakes and
Cumquat Marmalade

Contents

Metric Units

Many of the recipes in this book were written
before metric conversion. We have
left the measurements as we received them but provide the
following conversion table:

Length	1 in	= 25.4 mm	**Area**	1 in ^{2}	= 6.45 cm²
	1 in	= 2.54 cm		1 ft²	= 929 cm²
	1 ft	= 30.5 cm		1 yd²	= 0.836 m²
	1 yd	= 0.914 m		1 mile²	= 2.59 km²
	1 mile	= 1.61 km			
			Volume	1 fl oz	= 28.4 ml
Weight	1 oz	= 28.3 g		1 pint	= 568 ml
	1 lb	= 454 g		1 gal	= 4.55 litres

Introduction

THE IDEA FOR THE 'Q&A Cookbook' came from my editor, Nina Riemer. When she suggested it, I jumped at the idea. After all, there was a great deal of culinary material I had been unable to include in the three previous Q&A volumes and there were many variations of recipes submitted by Q&A listeners, excluded through lack of space. Here was another opportunity to prepare a book compiled from material so lovingly collected by so many people. It was apparent there would be great interest in a 'Q&A Cookbook' . . . food and its preparation had been a staple part of the program from Day One in October, 1982. So here is a collection of recipes from around the world—and from the private collections of some of the until now unheralded great cooks of Australia.

Throughout the collection there are recipes seemingly unconnected to particular questions. These were offered by listeners who discovered them while searching for something totally different, following an enquiry on the program, and who felt others might be interested. I'm glad they made that decision. Those recipes have added immensely to the scope and interest of this 'Q&A Cookbook'.

May I add that wherever possible I have tested the recipes in this book. A study of the lists of ingredients will make it obvious which recipes I have been unable to test-run.

Peter McCormack

Ginger Beer

Question Whenever I try to make a ginger beer plant, it just lies there and looks at me. I don't even get as far as having bottles of ginger beer blow up in the middle of the night. Where am I going wrong?

Answer Since the first Volume of *Q&A* we have had woeful stories of unsuccessful attempts at making ginger beer. Is there something mystical about ginger beer—some special quality necessary in the person who manufactures the delightful drink? Is it like making pastry? Do some people have the right touch while others rarely succeed? I like taking risks and I have included a number of recipes which the donors assure me will work. Every donor swears by his or her own special formula. Do try them, but do not come to me if you have not been successful. Neither have I!

AN OLD FAMILY RECIPE

1 Mix first four ingredients in a wide necked jar or similar container.
2 Allow to stand for three days.
3 Pour off almost all the liquid and feed the residue for four days with 1 teaspoon of sugar and 1 teaspoon of ground ginger.
4 After four days, stir vigourously and strain through muslin or nylon into a large container.
5 To the liquid add the sugar and water, dissolved together, the lemon juice and ground ginger.
6 Mix well.
7 Bottle and seal.

The ginger beer should be ready after ten days.

An Old Family Recipe: The Plant
½ **cup sugar**
1 dessertspoon ground ginger
juice of one lemon
1.1 litre water
additional sugar and ginger

The Ginger Beer:
4½ litres water
4 cups sugar
juice 4 lemons
2 tablespoons ground ginger

Ginger Beer

Subsequent Procedure

1 Return 'plant' residue to jar.
2 Add water.
3 Feed for 7 days with 1 teaspoon ginger and 1 teaspoon sugar.
4 Strain through muslin, reserving liquid and plant.

5 Make up liquid with sugar, water and lemon juice.
6 Mix well.
7 Bottle and seal.
8 Ready in 10 days.
9 Repeat ad nauseam.

Subsequent Procedure:

1½ cups water
7 teaspoons ginger
7 teaspoons sugar

3 cups sugar
1 gallon water (24 cups)
½ cup lemon juice

THE 1935 RECIPE

1 Cut lemons into thin slices and place in a large container.
2 Add sugar and bruised ginger.
3 Pour on boiling water.
4 Spread yeast on bread.
5 When liquid has cooled to blood heat, place bread/yeast on top and leave for 24 hours.
6 Strain into bottles, tie down securely.
7 Store for three to four days. Ginger beer should then be ready for use.

The 1935 Recipe:

2 lemons
450 g sugar
25 g yeast
1 slice bread
30 g fresh ginger
4½ litres boiling water

HONEY RAISIN GINGER BEER

1 Place all ingredients in a large jar with lid.
2 Shake thoroughly to dissolve sugar.
3 Leave in warm place until raisins float to top of liquid.
4 Strain through fine muslin or nylon and place sediment back in jar, discarding the raisins.
5 Add six more raisins, one teaspoon ginger, two heaped tablespoons sugar, juice of one lemon and 1.1 litre of water.
6 Leave as before until raisins rise to top of liquid then strain.
7 Plant (sediment) is now active.
8 Add one teaspoon ginger, two heaped tablespoons sugar, juice of one lemon, 1.1 litre of water.
9 Let stand for 48 hours.
10 Strain and pour into screwtop bottles.

Honey Raisin Ginger Beer:

1 cup sugar
10 raisins with seeds
1 tablespoon honey
juice 1 lemon
1 dessertspoon ground ginger
1.1 litre water

HOME STYLE GINGER BEER

Home Style Ginger Beer:
The Plant:

1 cup water
1 teaspoon ground ginger
1 teaspoon sugar
½ teaspoon instant coffee powder
1 teaspoon honey

The Ginger Beer:

3 cups sugar
4 cups hot water
4 litres cold water
½ cup strained lemon juice

1 Combine all ingredients in a screw top jar.
2 Feed plant each day for seven days with one teaspoon of sugar, one teaspoon of ground ginger, one teaspoon of honey, and half a teaspoon of instant coffee.

To Make Ginger Beer

1 Dissolve sugar in hot water.
2 Add cold water and strained lemon juice.
3 Add to this the strained liquid from the screwtop jar (strain through fine muslin).
4 Pour into clean, dry, airtight bottles and seal. Keep three to four weeks before using.

To keep the plant alive, halve the residue which was retained in the coth and return to jar with one cup of water. Let stand for one week, feeding daily as before.

OLD FASHIONED COUNTRY GINGER BEER

Country Ginger Beer:

Juice and peel one lemon
400 g sugar
30 g root ginger
boiling water
1 teaspoon dried powdered yeast

1 Peel the oily surfaces from a lemon and squeeze out the juice, putting both into a five-litre jug.
2 Add 400 g sugar and 30 g of well-bruised root ginger.
3 Fill jug with boiling water.
4 When cooled to blood heat, add dried powdered yeast and stir, but not enough to disturb the ginger.
5 After ten minutes in summer, or 30 minutes in winter (adjust accordingly to the season), bottle and seal. The last portions of the liquid should be strained through a cloth.
6 Leave bottles in a cool place for two to three days, when the ginger beer should be ready.

It is worth noting that ordinary corks will pop out under pressure. Better sealing methods are required.

Note: One listener has suggested adding a couple of grains of rice or wheat to the bottled ginger beer. But be careful! They do add fizz—but too many can add too much fizz.

PLANTLESS GINGER BEER

1 Dissolve the sugar in the nine litres of water.
2 Dissolve the remaining ingredients in the cup of water and allow to stand overnight.
3 Strain through fine cheesecloth, muslin, or nylon into screwtop bottles.
4 The ginger beer is ready in four to five days. It may be a good idea to store this bottling in the fridge after a couple of days to prevent explosions.

Plantless Ginger Beer:

1 kg sugar
9 litres water
1 cup water
1 teaspoon cream of tartar
1 teaspoon tartaric acid
1 teaspoon compressed yeast
1 tablespoon ground ginger
pinch salt

Boston Cream

Question Years ago, my aunt would make a fizzy drink at Christmas time. It had egg-whites in it, I think. I'd like the recipe.

Answer Boston Cream is an excellent non-alcoholic drink, suitable for summer. A good thirst quencher.

1 Place sugar and water in a large pan and bring to the boil.
2 Set aside to cool.
3 When quite cold, mix in the tartaric acid and lemon essence.
4 Fold in the beaten egg whites.
5 Beat all together
6 Bottle.

To use: 'Add half a tumblerful of cold water to a small wineglassful of the Boston Cream and add as much bicarbonate of soda as will cover a threepenny piece.* Stir and drink.'
The Cookery Book of Good and Tried Recipes, 1895

*A threepenny piece was roughly similar in size to a one cent piece

Boston Cream:

1400 g white sugar
4 litres water
45 g tartaric acid
1 tablespoon lemon essence
3 egg whites (beaten)

Lemon Beer

Lemon Beer:

1.4 kg sugar
4 tablespoons yeast
3 lemons, cut up
2 teaspoons cream of tartar
1 teaspoon tartaric acid
14 litres water
3 egg shells
30 g ground ginger

Question When I was a child I remember having a lemon drink at a cousin's farm. They called it lemon beer, but it wasn't alcoholic.

Answer Simple to make and quite refreshing, the traditional recipe calls for a four gallon kerosene tin, but a similarly sized container can be substituted.

Place all the ingredients in a container and let stand overnight. The next day strain and bottle your lemon beer.

Lemon Barley Water

Question Does someone have a recipe for lemon barley water?

Answer Here are two.

THICK BARLEY WATER

Thick Barley Water:

60 g pearl barley
5 litres water
zest of one lemon
sugar, if allowed

1 Wash barley well.
2 Put in pan with half the water and bring to the boil.
3 Discard the water and add remaining water.
4 Add lemon zest and simmer very gently for two hours.
5 Strain liquid into a jug through muslin and cool.
6 Stir occasionally while cooling.
7 Sweeten to taste with loaf sugar.

CLEAR BARLEY WATER

Clear Barley Water:

2 tablespoons pearl barley
rind of one lemon
3 lumps loaf sugar
1.2 litres boiling water
juice of half a lemon

1 Wash barley and place in jug with lemon rind.
2 Rub sugar on outside of lemon to extract oil from pith.
3 Drop sugar in jug.
4 Squeeze juice from lemon and add to jug.
5 Pour boiling water into jug and cover.
6 Stand jug in cool place for three hours, then strain liquid.

Parkin and Eccles Cakes

Question I would like the recipe for Parkin, which are English and come from the North Country. They're a cake or biscuit and they're made with oatmeal and treacle. I'd also like the recipe for Eccles cakes, which come from the North Country too. Eccles is a suburb of Manchester. Years ago I had the recipes, but lost them somewhere along the way.

Answer First—Eccles cakes and a little of their history. When the Puritans forbade dancing on the village green and all other public festivities, the eating of cakes at religious festivals was also forbidden. Eccles had a particularly stern parson, but perhaps he favoured Eccles cakes, for they continued to be baked. Today, there are several versions of Eccles cakes, one with short pastry, another with flaky pastry, both with various fillings. Here are two varieties:

ECCLES CAKES ONE

1 Roll the pastry to about a ½ cm thickness.
2 Use a cutter to stamp out rounds of pastry about 10 cm in diameter.
3 Warm the butter (make sure you do not let it melt) and mix with the sugar, mixed peel and currants.
4 Place a teaspoonful of this mixture in the centre of each round of pastry.
5 Wet the edges, draw together and seal in the centre with the fingers.
6 Turn the cake over and roll out until the filling can just be seen.
7 Make two or three cuts in the top.
8 Brush the top with egg white or water and sprinkle with caster sugar.
9 Bake in a 230°C oven for 20 minutes.

Eccles Cakes One:

230 g puff or flaky pastry
60 g butter
60 g brown sugar
60 g mixed peel
115 g currants
caster sugar
egg white

ECCLES CAKES TWO

Eccles Cakes Two:

short crust pastry
currants
golden syrup
desiccated coconut

1 Line patty-pans with pastry.
2 Pour in a layer of golden syrup, then a layer of currants. Top with desiccated coconut.
3 Cover with lid of pastry and bake.

Alternatively, you may line a baking pan with short crust pastry, put ingredients in layers as before and cover with more pastry. Mark the top lightly into finger sized pieces and bake. When cold, cut along the lines.

Fillings for both these versions of Eccles cakes can be enhanced by adding ground almonds, a little nutmeg and mace and a few drops of lemon juice.

'Parkin' seems to have originated in the late 1700s. Bad harvests had aggravated the economic problems brought about by the war with France. The turn of the century in Lancashire was a particularly bad time because few people could afford grain. Meal and corn were often 'off' and the use of treacle or syrup in the making of Parkin could have its origins in the days when treacle was used to sweeten sour oatmeal.

Parkin is made in Yorkshire and Lancashire at all times of the year, but especially for November the 5th, Guy Fawkes Day, at which time it is best eaten whilst standing around the bonfire, washed down with mugs of hot milk.

PARKIN ONE

Parkin One:

350 g lard
350 g butter
1 kg fine oatmeal
1 kg medium oatmeal
1 kg flour
2.5 kg treacle
4 eggs
30 g ground ginger
6 small teaspoons bicarb of soda
a glass of beer

1 Rub the lard and butter into the oatmeals and flour.
2 Warm the treacle and pour into the dry ingredients.
3 Stir in eggs and ginger to make a good dough.
4 Dissolve bicarb soda in the beer and add to the dough.
5 Mix well. The dough should drop, not run, off the spoon.
6 Bake in well-buttered tins, making sure not to fill them too high. The oven should not be too hot, as the Parkin will quickly burn.

PARKIN TWO

1 Mix together flour, salt, oatmeal and ginger.
2 Melt sugar, lard and syrup and add a little of the milk.
3 Pour this into the flour mixture and stir to a stiff batter.
4 Dissolve bicarb soda in remaining milk and add to batter.
5 Mix quickly and pour into a shallow tin, which has been lined with greased paper.
6 Bake for one hour and twenty minutes at 120°C. Parkin should never be overbaked or it will be dry. Parkin should always be allowed to 'come' again in its tin before being eaten. Allow as long as possible between baking day and eating day. The result will be a dark crumbling stickiness that melts in the mouth.

Parkin Two:
230 g plain flour
pinch salt
230 g medium oatmeal
½ teaspoon ground ginger
115 g sugar
100 g lard
280 g golden syrup
150 ml milk
1 teaspoon bicarb of soda

Welsh Buns

Question I heard the question about Eccles cakes and it reminded me of something I had years ago—Welsh buns. I'd like to try making them.

Answer This is the recipe for Welsh buns—or *Buns Cymreig*.

1 Cream the butter and sugar.
2 Add well beaten egg yolks and mix thoroughly.
3 Gradually beat in the flour.
4 Add the sultanas or currants.
5 Beat egg whites to a stiff froth and add to mixture.
6 Beat all thoroughly for 20 to 30 minutes.
7 Shape dough into buns about the size of an egg or pour the mixture into a greased tin.
8 Bake in a slow oven (150°C) for two and a half to three hours until lightly browned.

Welsh Buns:
230 g butter
175 g sugar
3 eggs, separated
450 g self raising flour
230 g sultanas or currants

Welsh Cakes

Question I married a Welshman and I'm not complaining about that but he keeps asking for Welsh cakes. I tried the recipes for Welsh buns and Eccles cakes which were in *Q&A* Volume One, but he says they're not Welsh cakes. Does someone have the recipe for the 'real' thing?

Answer Here's a recipe for the 'real' thing from a 'Williams of Llanelli'. Welsh cakes are described as being similar to pikelets but in appearance only. They are made from a dough containing sultanas. They are definitely not 'singing hinnies' which are from Northumberland (see below). True Welsh cakes should be made on a griddle but an electric frypan can be used successfully.

Welsh Cakes:
115 g butter
3 cups self raising flour
pinch of salt
1 cup sugar
1 cup sultanas
1 egg
½ cup milk

1 Rub softened butter into flour until the whole resembles fine bread crumbs.
2 Stir in salt, sugar and sultanas.
3 Beat together the egg and half the milk.
4 Stir the egg/milk into the dry ingredients, adding sufficient of the remaining milk to form a moist but not sticky dough.
5 Turn onto a floured surface and knead lightly.
6 Press out to approximately 1 cm thick and cut into rounds with a scone cutter.
7 Cook on a lightly greased griddle over medium heat or use a lightly greased electric frypan at 180°C. Cook the Welsh cakes in small batches for about three minutes per side. Serve with butter.

SINGING HINNIES

Singing Hinnies:
350 g plain flour
60 g ground rice
pinch of salt
60 g sugar
2 teaspoons baking powder
30 g shortening
100 g currants
290 ml liquid (½ milk, ½ cream)

1 Mix flour, ground rice, salt, sugar and baking powder and rub in shortening.
2 Mix in currants, which have been washed and dried.
3 Add liquid and mix to a moderately soft dough.
4 Roll out to 1 cm thickness.
5 Prick all over with a fork.
6 Bake on a fairly hot griddle to brown both sides. Cut into halves or quarters for turning.

Split, butter and eat hot.

World's Best Chocolate Cake

Question I'm after the recipe for what has been described as the world's best chocolate cake—the *Sacher Torte*. I believe it contains about a kilogram of chocolate.

Answer The flood of response to this request indicated that many people regard the *Sacher Torte* as truly the best chocolate cake in the world. There seems to be some argument, however, as to the true recipe. This was developed at one of Vienna's hotels, The Sacher, by the jovial Frau Sacher. She owned the hotel at the time of the Emperor Franz Josef. Here is a recipe that may be close to the real thing, but be warned that it calls for an old fashioned half hour creaming of the butter with the yolks of the eggs and the sugar. However, it does *not* require one kilo of chocolate.

1 Cream the butter with the caster sugar and egg yolks until light and smooth (about half an hour).
2 Beat egg whites until stiff (the egg whites, that is), then add the 110 gm of sugar gradually, continuing to beat.
3 Fold a spoonful of flour to a spoonful of egg white into the egg yolk/sugar/butter mixture, taking care to keep the whole as light as possible. The egg whites are the aerating agent.
4 Melt the chocolate over hot water with a little rum and then cool.
5 Add to cake mixture.
6 Grease the bottom of a 22 cm pan and line it with greased paper.
7 Pour the mixture into the pan and smooth top.
8 Bake in preheated 170°C oven for 12 minutes with the door slightly open.
9 Close oven door and bake for a further one hour.
10 When cake is done, remove from oven, carefully run a knife around the edges and turn out onto a wire rack.

World's Best Chocolate Cake:

130 g unsalted butter
110 g caster sugar
6 egg yolks
6 egg whites
130 g cooking chocolate
110 g sugar
130 g flour
a little rum
raspberry jam
chocolate glaze

11 Gently remove paper.
12 When cake is cool, spread top with raspberry jam and cover with a chocolate glaze, made with cocoa, sugar and water.
13 Let stand overnight.
14 Serve with whipped cream.

Our correspondents report that it may be difficult to achieve success with this cake.

THE SEARCH CONTINUES

The Search Continues:

145 g butter
145 g sugar
145 g chocolate
8 egg yolks
10 egg whites
115 g flour
60 g apricot jam
Chocolate Icing:
170 g sugar
water
170 g best plain chocolate

1 Beat the butter until quite fluffy.
2 Melt chocolate in oven and add to the creamed butter together with the sugar.
3 Add the egg yolks one after the other.
4 Whisk the egg whites until stiff, then fold in the flour.
5 Add this to the first mixture.
6 Butter a cake tin, flour it lightly and pour in the cake mixture.
7 Bake slowly in a medium oven for one and a half hours.
8 Remove from oven, turn out onto a wire rack, then immediately invert onto another rack, as it is essential that this cake cools in the same position in which it was baked.
9 When the cake has cooled, cut the top level, then invert again.
10 Warm the apricot jam a little and spread over the cake.
11 Cover with chocolate icing.

Chocolate Icing:
1 Bring sugar to boil with a little less than half a cup of water.
2 Cook syrup until it forms a thin thread at the end of a wooden spoon.
3 Add the melted chocolate and mix well, making sure there are no lumps.
4 Keep stirring the frosting until the mixture is thick enough to pour over the cake.
5 Allow the icing to set.
6 Serve the cake with whipped cream in a separate bowl.

IS THIS THE WORLD'S BEST?

1   Combine butter and caster sugar and mix until light and creamy.
2   Add egg yolks one by one, beating well.
3   Cut the vanilla beans lengthwise, scrape out the inside and combine this with the butter/sugar/egg mixture.
4   Break the cooking chocolate into small pieces and melt it in a double boiler over warm water.
5   Add the melted chocolate to the butter/sugar/egg mixture.
6   Beat the egg whites until stiff then add the 110 g of sugar slowly until you achieve a meringue.
7   Fold this meringue and the flour into the egg yolk mixture.
8   Grease the bottom of a 22 cm springform pan, line it with paper and then grease the paper.
9   Pour the cake mixture into the pan and smooth the top.
10 Bake the cake in a preheated 150° to 175°C oven for 12 minutes, with the door of the oven slightly open, then for one hour with the door closed.
11 When the baking time is over, remove the pan from the oven, carefully run a knife around the edges of the cake and remove springform ring.
12 Turn the cake onto a wire rack to cool and remove the paper.
13 Put the apricot jam through a sieve and heat in a small pan.
14 Brush the top and sides of the cake with the warm jam and allow to dry.
15 Boil the 125 ml of water and the 200 g of sugar for five minutes, then allow to cool.
16 Break the eating chocolate into small pieces and gently stir it into the sugar syrup until it is completely dissolved.
17 Reserve about 60 ml of this chocolate/syrup mixture. Pour the rest over the cake and spread it carefully over the top and sides with a spatula. Work quickly.
18 With a piping bag and the finest nozzle, use the reserved 60 ml of chocolate mixture to mark 16 slices on the top of the cake.

Is This the World's Best?

130 g butter
110 g caster sugar
6 egg yolks
2 vanilla beans
130 g cooking chocolate
6 egg whites
110 g sugar
130 g flour
100 ml apricot jam
125 ml water
200 g sugar
150 g dark eating chocolate

MAYBE THIS IS THE BEST

Maybe This is the Best

225 g unsweetened chocolate
200 g butter
240 g confectioners sugar
8 egg yolks, well beaten
⅔ cup fine dry bread crumbs
8 egg whites
⅛ teaspoon salt
200 g apricot conserve, pureed and heated
icing for decoration

1 Grease bottom of 22 cm springform pan and line bottom with waxed paper.
2 Melt chocolate and set aside to cool.
3 Cream butter in a large mixer bowl until softened.
4 Beat in 120 g of the sugar until mixture is fluffy.
5 Gradually add egg yolks, beating well after each addition.
6 Blend in the chocolate and the crumbs.
7 Beat egg whites with the salt until frothy.
8 Add remaining 120 g sugar, several tablespoons at a time, beating constantly until peaks are formed.
9 Spread egg yolk mixture over the egg whites and fold together.
10 Turn batter into springform pan.
11 Bake in a moderate 180°C oven for 50 to 60 minutes.
12 Remove from the oven and place on a wire rack to cool completely.
13 Carefully loosen sides of cake with a spatula and remove cake from pan. Peel off the waxed paper.
14 Spread torte with heated pureed apricot preserve and allow to cool.
15 Cover with chocolate frosting.

Chocolate Frosting: Partially melt 85 g of semi-sweet chocolate, then remove from heat and stir until completely melted. Add 100 g of unsalted butter and stir until it too is melted. If desired, mark the surface of the Torte into 12 parts and decorate each with the name *Sacher*, in sugar icing.

OR IS IT THIS ONE?

Or is This the One?:

250 g dark chocolate
1 cup SR flour
250 g butter
6 eggs, separated
125 g ground almonds
125 g rum
125 g red currant jelly
1 cup caster sugar

1 Chop chocolate roughly and combine with the butter in the top of a double boiler.
2 Stir till melted then cool to lukewarm.
3 Beat egg yolks and sugar until thick and creamy.
4 Add ground almonds and sifted flour and mix.
5 Stir in cooked chocolate mixture.
6 Beat egg whites until stiff peaks form.
7 Fold into mixture gently but thoroughly.

8 Spoon into two greased 20 cm sandwich tins and bake in a moderate oven for 20 to 25 minutes.
9 Turn onto a wire rack to cool.
10 When cold, split each layer into two.
11 Place one top layer aside, and then carefully assemble the remaining three layers, brushing each with the rum, then with a thin layer of the red currant jelly.
12 Place the top layer in position and spread icing evenly over the top and sides of the cake.

Icing: Combine 185 g of roughly chopped chocolate with 60 g of butter in the top of a double saucepan over hot water. Stir until melted.

SWISS CHOCOLATE CAKE

The difficulty of achieving success with the *Sacher Torte* recipe (it has defeated some of the best cake makers) prompts me to suggest you might like to try this traditional Swiss recipe which has been handed down through generations and passed to *Q&A* by a generous listener. Although expensive, it is absolutely delicious.

1 Melt chocolate in pan with a little water.
2 Cream butter, sugar and egg yolks for about 20 minutes.
3 Add almond meal, crushed biscuits and melted chocolate. Mix well.
4 Fold in egg whites at the end. This makes a very thick mixture.
5 Bake at 180°C for about 45 minutes in a large flat tin (a pizza pan is ideal). An ordinary cake tin will not allow the cake to set properly in the middle.
6 Leave to cool and turn out very carefully, if using the pizza pan, otherwise it may break in the middle.
7 Before serving dredge with icing sugar.

This cake is best left a day or two before eating— if you can resist the temptation.

Swiss Chocolate Cake:

250 g chocolate (not cooking chocolate)

150 g butter

250 g caster sugar

6 egg yolks

125 g almond meal

75 g crushed Savoiardi biscuits

6 egg whites, stiffly beaten

Sour Cream Cake

Question I have a recipe for a sour cream cake, but I'm not sure exactly when the sultanas should be added. I believe this is crucial to the success of the cake.

Answer The sultanas go in last!

Sour Cream Cake:
½ cup butter
1 cup caster sugar
2 eggs
2 cups SR flour
¾ cup sultanas
1 level teaspoon cinnamon
grated rind 1 lemon
¾ cup sour cream

1 Cream the butter and sugar until fluffy.
2 Add eggs and beat well.
3 Sift flour.
4 Sprinkle one tablespoon of the flour over the sultanas.
5 Add remaining flour to the butter/sugar/egg mixture, alternately with the sour cream.
6 Add floured sultanas and grated lemon rind.
7 Pour into floured 23 cm square or round tin.
8 Bake in a moderate (180°C) oven for about one hour.
9 Allow to cool in tin.

Note: If sultanas, or other dried fruits, are floured, they are less likely to sink to the bottom of the cake as it is cooked.

SOUR CREAM AND HONEY LOAF

Sour Cream & Honey Loaf:
110 ml sour cream
115 g brown sugar
1 large egg
260 g wholemeal flour
1 level tablespoon bicarb
2 level teaspoons ground cinnamon
60 g fruit or nuts
4 tablespoons honey
85 g margarine

1 Set oven to 150°C.
2 Place sour cream in bowl.
3 Beat in sugar and egg.
4 Add sifted flour and mix.
5 Add bicarb, cinnamon and nuts or fruit.
6 Gently heat honey and margarine until melted.
7 Stir this into the flour mixture.
8 Transfer to greased 1 kg loaf tin, lined on base.
9 Bake in centre of a moderate (180°C) oven for one and a half hours, or until cooked.
10 Cool in the tin.

Pavlova

In 1985 the old argument about the origin of the Pavlova surfaced yet again. Was it created first in Australia, or across the Tasman in New Zealand?

The Australian proponents maintain that the Pavlova was created by a Perth chef, Herbert Sachse, in honour of Anna Pavlova's visit in 1925. The New Zealanders say that a South Island housewife was making the concoction ten years earlier. My vote goes to the Sachse creation—after all it is called Pavlova, and known by that name.

Herbert Sachse's homage to the great Russian ballerina has a thin biscuit coloured crust and the rest is almost entirely a marshmallow-like centre. The concoction from the Land of the Long White Cloud is all white, crisp meringue on the outside and soft in the centre.

TRADITIONAL PAV

1 Beat egg whites until stiff and solid.
2 Add 2 tablespoons of caster sugar and beat well.
3 Add the remainder of the sugar gradually, beating briskly all the time.
4 Fold in the flavouring, vinegar and cornflour without beating, but make sure they are mixed evenly throughout.
5 Line a 20 cm springform tin with waxed paper on both the bottom and the sides.
6 Spread a layer of the meringue mixture on the bottom, then swirl the remainder around the sides and towards the middle, leaving a hollow in the centre.
7 Bake in the middle of a very moderate (150°C) oven for about one and a quarter hours, at which time the pavlova should be crisp on the outside, but still soft in the middle.
8 Leave to cool, then remove from the tin.
9 Spread a little of the whipped cream around the outside of the pavlova, then roll in chopped nuts.
10 Place on the serving plate and fill the centre with the remaining whipped cream and the fruits. Decorate with small leaves of angelica.

Traditional Pav:

3 egg whites

180 g caster sugar

1 teaspoon vanilla essence

1 teaspoon vinegar

1 teaspoon cornflour

2 tablespoons chopped roasted almonds

300 ml double cream, whipped, flavoured with vanilla and sweetened with 1 teaspoon caster sugar

soft fruits in season

angelica

Pavlova

OZ PAV

1 Sift the cornflour and caster sugar together three times.
2 Line the base and sides of a 20 cm deep sided round tin with brown paper. Grease the sides lightly with butter.
3 Mix the extra cornflour and caster sugar together and sprinkle half over base.
4 Preheat oven to 260°C.
5 Beat the egg whites until they are stiff, adding the cream of tartar and the vanilla essence.
6 Lightly fold in the sifted sugar and cornflour.
7 Fold in the vinegar.
8 Spread in the prepared tin.
9 Sprinkle remaining cornflour/sugar mixture over the top.
10 Place on the middle shelf of the oven and immediately turn the heat as low as it will go. Bake for 15 minutes and check for any browning.
11 If tinted, turn off the heat for 15 minutes, then relight oven and bake for at least one and a half hours. Check for browning.
12 Turn out onto a cake cooler which has been covered with greaseproof paper. Peel off the lining paper and allow to cool.
13 Use your favourite fruit fillings.

Oz Pav:

6 egg whites

pinch of cream of tartar

a few drops of vanilla essence

¾ cup caster sugar

4 tablespoons cornflour

2 teaspoons white vinegar

2 tablespoons each of extra sugar and cornflour

ENZED PAV

1 Line a baking tray with greaseproof paper and mark out a 20 cm circle.
2 Beat the egg whites until soft peaks form.
3 Add the sugar, one tablespoon at a time, beating for half a minute after each addition.
4 Fold in the cornflour and then the vinegar.
5 Brush the marked circle lightly with a little water and spread the meringue mixture in the circle, making a hollow in the centre.
6 Bake in the cool part of a slow (150°C) oven for about one and a half hours, until the pav is firm to the touch.
7 Turn off the heat and allow the pav to remain in the oven with the door open until it is cold.
8 Peel off paper before serving.

Enzed Pav:

4 egg whites

1 cup caster sugar

2 teaspoons cornflour

2 teaspoons white vinegar

Paskha

Question Years ago I tasted a delicious dessert which was made with cream cheese and other ingredients. At the time I was told it was a typical Russian dessert served at Easter. As I do not know its name I am unable to track it down.

Answer The dessert is Russian. It is an integral part of Easter feasting and is called Paskha. A special pyramid-shaped paskha mould is used to make the dessert, but a flower pot or a colander may be substituted. In this recipe, cottage cheese may be used instead of cream cheese.

Pashka:

1 kg cream cheese
3 tablespoons sultanas
120 g softened butter
2 tablespoons raisins
120 ml sour cream
2 tablespoons slivered almonds
120 g sugar
1 tablespoon toasted slivered almonds
1 egg yolk
1 tablespoon chopped glace cherries
½ teaspoon vanilla
very finely grated rind one lemon

1 Place the cream cheese in a large wire strainer over a mixing bowl. Cover the cheese with a clean cloth and place a heavy weight on top. Leave to drain for at least two hours.
2 Discard the liquid.
3 Place the cheese in a mixing bowl and beat in the softened butter—a little at a time—until well blended.
4 In a medium size bowl combine the sour cream, sugar and egg yolk, beating until the sugar has dissolved.
5 Gradually add the sour cream mixture to the cream cheese/butter mix, beating constantly.
6 Add the vanilla and the grated lemon rind.
7 Fold in the sultanas and raisins, almonds, toasted almonds and cherries.
8 Line the paskha mould (or use a flowerpot or colander) with cheesecloth or muslin.
9 Spoon in the mixture and smooth the top.
10 Cover the mould with a clean, damp cloth and place a heavy weight on top.
11 Place the lot in the refrigerator and chill for at least eight hours, or overnight.
12 To serve—remove the weight and top cloth. Place an inverted serving dish over the mould and with a sharp shake turn out dessert.
13 Remove and discard cheesecloth.
14 The paskha is now ready to be decorated with nuts and crystallised fruit.

Lemon Butter Sponge

Question One of my aunts had a speciality—lemon butter sponge—which made my mouth water (the memory of it still does). Unfortunately she's no longer with us. Would someone have the recipe?

Answer Here are a few including this very old recipe which is thought to have come from Mrs Ada Henningham, who worked for the Anthill family at Picton after her arrival in Australia from Birmingham, England.

1 Cream sugar with butter.
2 Add flour, juice and rind of lemon, milk.
3 Separate egg yolks and whites.
4 Beat in egg yolks.
5 Beat egg whites until stiff but not dry.
6 Fold whites into mixture.
7 Pour into piedish, stand in dish of cold water and cook slowly.

LEMON SPONGE

1 Sift flour, baking powder and salt three or four times.
2 Separate egg yolks and whites.
3 Beat yolks and lemon rind until thick and creamy.
4 Beat in lemon juice.
5 Whisk egg whites to a stiff but not dry froth.
6 Gradually whisk in the sugar.
7 When quite smooth and creamy thoroughly mix in the beaten egg yolks.
8 Gradually fold in the sifted flour.
9 Grease two sandwich tins.
10 Pour in the mixture and bake in a moderate oven for 20 to 25 minutes.
11 Remove from tins and fill with lemon butter (see below).
12 Pipe fresh cream around top.

Lemon Butter:

1 Cook all ingredients together over boiling water until the mixture is the consistency of honey.
2 Stir occasionally.

Lemon Butter Sponge:

1 cup sugar
1 tablespoon butter
2 tablespoons self-raising flour
juice and rind of 1 lemon
2 cups milk
2 eggs

Lemon Sponge:

1 cup plain flour
2 level teaspoons baking powder
¼ level teaspoon salt
4 eggs
1 cup sugar
1 teaspoon grated lemon rind
1½ tablespoons lemon juice

Lemon Butter:

90 g sugar
⅓ cup lemon juice
30 g butter
1 egg yolk
1 level teaspoon grated lemon rind

LEMON DELICIOUS PUDDING

Lemon Delicious Pudding:

3 eggs
½ cup sugar
1 cup milk
1 tablespoon SR flour
1 tablespoon grated lemon rind
½ cup lemon juice
pinch salt
1 tablespoon sugar, extra

1 Separate eggs and beat yolks with half a cup of sugar until light and creamy.
2 Beat in milk, sifted flour, lemon rind and juice, and salt.
3 Beat egg whites until soft peaks form and fold into lemon mixture.
4 Pour into a greased, deep, one-litre ovenproof dish. Stand this dish in a shallow pan of cold water and sprinkle top with one tablespoon of sugar.
5 Bake in a moderate oven for 50 to 60 minutes.

Serves four

LEMON BUTTER CAKE

Lemon Butter:

60 g butter
1 cup sugar
2 lemons
2 eggs

Cake Mixture:

125 g butter
¼ cup sugar
1 egg
1 cup SR flour
½ cup plain flour
pinch salt
¼ cup blanched almonds

To make lemon butter:
1 Place butter, sugar, beaten eggs, grated rind of one lemon and strained juice of both lemons in the top of a double boiler.
2 Place over boiling water and stir with a wooden spoon while cooking until thickened. This should take about 20 minutes. Cool the lemon butter.

To make the cake:
1 Cream the butter and sugar.
2 Add the egg and beat well.
3 Add the sifted flours and salt and mix.
4 Knead on a floured board and divide in two.
5 Roll out to fit one 20 cm cake tin.
6 Put one part of cake mixture in the tin and press over the base and up the sides.
7 Spread the lemon butter mixture over this, using about half the quantity.
8 Put the other section of the rolled out cake mixture on the top.
9 Decorate with halved blanched almonds and sprinkle lightly with sugar.
10 Bake in a moderately hot (200°C) oven for 40 minutes or until lightly browned.

Serve with whipped cream.

Jersey Wonders

Question While on a trip to Britain, I was served some delicious cakes called Jersey Wonders. How do I make them?

Answer Jersey Wonders are an Easter treat, also known as *Des Merveilles*.

1 Sift the flours together in a bowl.
2 Add the sugar and rub in the butter.
3 Add enough of the beaten egg to give a fairly stiff dough. Do not overwork the mixture.
4 Divide into 20 pieces and roll into walnut-sized balls.
5 Allow to stand for 30 minutes.
6 Roll each into an oblong about 8 cm by 4 cm, handling very lightly.
7 Make two slits lengthwise. This will make three bands. Tuck the ends through the slits making a figure-of-eight or bow shape.
8 Heat oil to 185°C and fry quickly, turning if necessary until golden brown. Do a few at a time, depending on the size of the pan.
9 Lift out with a slotted spoon and drain on absorbent kitchen paper.
10 Serve dredged with icing sugar or cinnamon sugar, or with raspberry, plum or apricot sauce.

Jersey Wonders:

175 g self raising flour

50 g plain flour

50 g sugar

50 g butter

2 small eggs (beaten)

oil for deep frying

Puftaloons

Question Is there something called hot daloonies? I've been told they're a fried scone.

Answer The fried scones are called puftaloons. They are usually served hot with golden syrup and they disappear as fast as they are made.

1 Sift dry ingredients together.
2 Add enough milk to make a soft sough.
3 Knead slightly and roll out to about 1 cm thick.
4 Cut into rounds.

Puftaloons:

1 cup plain flour

pinch salt

1 teaspoon baking powder

milk

clarified fat

5 Drop into hot, deep fat, until the puftaloons are golden brown and puffed.

6 Serve with golden syrup, or sprinkle with sugar and serve with jam.

When properly cooked, puftaloons are hollow inside.

PUFTALOONS TWO

Puftaloons Two:
1 cup SR flour
140 ml milk
pinch salt

1 Mix into a light dough and knead lightly.
2 Cut into rounds 50 mm thick.
3 Heat fat in a pan.
4 When fat begins to smoke slightly, reduce heat and fry rounds until they are golden brown on both sides. Use a knife or spatula to turn. Do **not** cook quickly or the centre will be soft. The rounds should be thin as they rise a lot.
5 Drain on kitchen paper.
6 Serve at once with jam or honey, or for breakfast garnish with bacon.

Buckwheat Pancakes

Southern Buckwheat Pancakes:
½ cup sifted plain flour
½ teaspoon baking powder
½ teaspoon salt
1 teaspoon bicarb soda
1½ cups buckwheat flour
1¼ cups buttermilk
1 tablespoon table molasses
2 tablespoons melted butter

Question I've just returned from a holiday in America. I thought I might overdose on pancakes while I was there, but I still have a hankering for some—particularly buckwheat pancakes. Is making them much different to making ordinary pancakes?

Answer No, not really. Try one of these.

1 Let griddle heat slowly.
2 Sift flour with baking powder, salt, bicarb soda and stir in buckwheat flour.
3 Pour buttermilk and molasses into mixing bowl and stir in melted butter.
4 Add dry ingredients, stirring only until well blended.
5 Place batter, by the spoonful, on the hot griddle.
6 Turn pancakes once to brown on both sides, then serve piping hot.

This amount makes 12 to 16 pancakes.

BRETON BUCKWHEAT PANCAKES

1 Mix together the oil, brandy, salt, buttermilk and flour.
2 Add eggs, one by one, working mixture well to avoid lumps.
3 Cook pancakes on a griddle which has been rubbed with butter or fat.

Breton Pancakes:

500 g buckwheat flour
2 small glasses brandy
2 pinches salt
2 cups curdled milk or buttermilk
8 whole eggs
2 tablespoons olive oil

LIGHT BUCKWHEAT CAKES

This batter is so light that it makes a lot of pancakes. It keeps well, covered, in the refrigerator for several days.

Sift flour before measuring. Resift with baking powder, salt, bicarb and sugar. Add buckwheat flour. Pour buttermilk into bowl. Add shortening. Add the dry ingredients. Beat the batter until it is blended only. Drop onto heated griddle or pan, cook two to three minutes, then turn and leave until cooked.

Light Buckwheat Cakes:

½ cup all-purpose flour
½ teaspoon double-acting baking powder
½ teaspoon salt
1 teaspoon bicarb soda
2 teaspoons sugar
1½ cups buckwheat flour
3¼ cups buttermilk
2 tablespoons melted shortening

BUTTERMILK WAFFLES

1 Cook the meal, water, salt and shortening together for ten minutes, stirring constantly.
2 Beat the egg yolks and the whites separately until very light.
3 When corn mush is cool add the yolks.
4 Sift together the soda and the flour and add to corn mush, alternating with the sweet milk.
5 Fold in the beaten egg whites.
6 Finally add enough buttermilk to make a pouring batter.
7 Bake in a hot waffle iron.

Note: This mixture is improved if it stands for a short time before the waffles are baked.

Buttermilk Waffles:

1 cup corn meal
1½ cups water
1 teaspoon salt
1 tablespoon shortening
2 eggs
1 cup wheat flour
¾ teaspoon bicarb soda
½ cup milk
buttermilk

BAKING POWDER BUCKWHEAT CAKES

Buckwheat Cakes:

1½ cups buckwheat flour
½ cup wheat flour
5 teaspoons baking powder
½ teaspoon salt
1 tablespoon shortening
1 tablespoon molasses
1½ cups milk

1 Sift dry ingredients together.
2 Add melted shortening to milk and molasses.
3 Add liquid to dry ingredients and beat well.
4 Cook until browned on both sides on a slightly greased hot griddle.

Friendship Cake

Friendship Cake:

1 cup sugar—white, raw or brown
5-6 cups dried fruits—raisins, dried apple, nuts, apricots, cherries, or chopped mixed fruit
3 eggs, beaten
⅔ cup oil or melted butter
2 teaspoons vanilla
2 cups plain flour
1½ teaspoons cinnamon
¾ teaspoon nutmeg
½ teaspoon salt
1½ teaspoons bicarb soda
2 teaspoons baking powder
Topping:
½ cup soft butter
1 cup brown sugar
1 teaspoon cinnamon
1 teaspoon plain flour

Question Does anyone have the recipe for the Friendship Cake, including the 'starter' which one can pass on to friends?

Answer *Starter—the first day:* In a bowl place one cup each of sugar, plain flour and milk. If you wish to pass on the starter and recipe to three friends, add to your own starter on *the first day* and the *fifth day*, one cup each of the ingredients. Stir each day for *ten days*. The mixture will rise in the bowl like yeast and will subside when stirred. On *the tenth day* take out three separate cups of the mixture and place in three screwtop jars. Give these together with the recipe to three friends (or keep one for yourself). **Do not refrigerate.**

1 Grease and flour a large cake tin or two 20 cm tins.
2 Beat together the sugar, eggs, oil or butter, vanilla, flour.
3 Add to starter.
4 Add remaining ingredients and mix.
5 Bake at 140°C for approximately one and a half hours.
6 Remove from tin while still hot.

Topping:
1 Mix ingredients together.
2 Smooth over top of cake.
3 Place under griller.

Alice's Christmas Cake

While we are on the subject of Christmas, here's the recipe for the Christmas Cake made so elegantly for many, many years by my mother, Alice McCormack.

1 Cream the butter and sugar.
2 Add eggs, one at a time.
3 Add sherry.
4 Add half the dried fruit.
5 Twice sift together the flour, bicarb soda, and spices and add to mixture.
6 Add remainder of the flour and fruit to the mixture, the raisins and cherries having been chopped into small pieces.
7 Place the lot in an 8 inch (20 cm) tin, which has been lined with three thicknesses of brown paper.
8 Cook in preheated 325°F (160°C) oven for half an hour, then reduce heat to 275°F (140°C) and cook cake for a further three and a half to four hours.
9 Remove cake from oven, rest for half an hour then carefully dribble one tablespoon of sherry over the top.

My mother usually makes the cake(s) about the middle of the year and adds a little sherry every month. She makes small holes with a fine skewer around the top of the cake before adding the extra sherry.

Alice's Christmas Cake:

250 g butter
250 g caster sugar
5 eggs
310 g plain flour
½ teaspoon bicarb soda
1 teaspoon mixed spice
1 teaspoon cinnamon
185 g mixed peel
185 g currants
500 g raisins
500 g sultanas
30 g glace cherries
50 ml sherry

Vanochka (the Czech Christmas Plait)

Vanochka:
450 g white bread flour
1 teaspoon salt
115 g vanilla sugar
2 egg yolks, beaten
30 g fresh yeast
275 ml warm milk
30 g chopped mixed peel
30 g sultanas
115 g melted butter
55 g flaked almonds
Topping:
2 egg whites, beaten
pinch of salt
1 or 2 tablspoons flaked almonds or 30 g poppy seeds

Question I once experienced the pleasure of sharing a special European Christmas treat. It was a plaited and decorated bread. I would like the recipe.

Answer The special Christmas bread is called *Vanochka*. It originates in Czechoslovakia.

1 Sift flour and salt into a large bowl.
2 In a smaller bowl put a quarter of the sifted flour, 30 g of the sugar, the two egg yolks, the yeast and half the warm milk and beat well to a smooth batter, entirely free of lumps.
3 Cover the bowl with a cloth and allow to stand until the mixture is light and spongy.
4 Meanwhile, soak the mixed peel and sultanas in the rest of the warm milk.
5 Add the butter, the almonds, remaining sugar and the soaked fruit to the sifted flour, together with the yeast mixture and enough of the warm milk to make a manageable dough which is kneaded on a floured board until it is smooth and elastic.
6 Place the dough in a large greased polythene bag, cover it with a cloth and prove until it has doubled its size.
7 Punch down the dough on a floured board and divide it into eight equal pieces.
8 Put four of the pieces back into the polythene bag and roll the other four pieces into long ropes.
9 Plait these, starting in the middle. Damp the ends with water and pinch together to prevent separating. This section forms the base of the loaf.
10 Place this plait on a greased baking sheet and brush with the egg whites which have been beaten a little with a pinch of salt.
11 Make another plait with three of the remaining pieces of dough, place this firmly on top of the first plait and brush also with the beaten egg white.

12 Divide the last piece of dough into two and roll into two thin ropes. Twist these together and press along the top of the last plait.
13 Brush with egg white. If the first two plaits look dry, brush them again with the egg white.
14 Sprinkle loaf with poppy seeds or flaked almonds and cover with cloth and allow to stand until well risen.
15 Bake in a moderate (180°C) oven for 40 to 45 minutes, until golden brown.
16 Halfway through the cooking, if the loaf is decorated with almonds, cover the loaf loosely with a piece of greaseproof paper to prevent the almonds burning.
17 Cook on a wire rack before serving.

The Food of Angels

Question When I was quite young my mother baked Angel's Food cake for the family. We loved it then—it was a special treat. I'd like the recipe.

Answer This request resulted in recipes for Angel's Food Cake and also for a dessert called Angel's Food and for Angel Food Fudge.

ANGEL'S FOOD CAKE

1 Sift the two flours, salt, baking powder and cream of tartar three times, and place in a large bowl.
2 Beat the egg whites until they are stiff. Turn the mixer to its lowest speed, add the vanilla and sugar, beating until just combined.
3 Fold this mixture into the dry ingredients and pour into an ungreased 23 cm tube cake tin.
4 Bake in a moderately slow oven (180°C) for 50 to 60 minutes until the cake is golden brown and feels set, as when testing a sponge.
5 Remove from the oven and place the inverted cake on a cooler. Let stand for about an hour.
6 Loosen the cake from the tin with a sharp knife and tap it from the tin.
7 Serve frosted, or with cream and fresh fruits as a dessert.

Angel's Food Cake:

¾ **cup flour**

⅔ **cup cornflour**

¼ **level teaspoon salt**

2 **level teaspoons baking powder**

2 **level teaspoons cream of tartar**

10 **egg whites**

1⅓ **cups caster sugar**

1 **teaspoon vanilla**

ANGEL'S FOOD PUDDING

Angel's Food Pudding:

1 egg
3 teaspoons gelatine
1 cup milk
2 tablespoons hot water
1 tablespoon sugar
3 drops vanilla essence

1 Separate white from yolk of egg.
2 Heat milk and sugar, pour gently onto egg yolk and mix well.
3 Return to saucepan, heat gently, stirring well without boiling until mixture coats spoon.
4 Cool.
5 Dissolve gelatine in hot water. Add to cool custard mixture, together with the vanilla.
6 Beat egg white until stiff and fold lightly into mixture.
7 Pour into wet mould and set.
8 Turn out onto serving dish.

LEMON ANGEL'S FOOD

Lemon Angel's Food:

30 g gelatine
1¼ litres milk
3 or 4 eggs (separated)
½ cup sugar
1 or 2 lemons
vanilla

1 Soak the gelatine in a third of the milk till soft.
2 Boil the rest of the milk, add the gelatine and the sugar and boil.
3 Stir in the yolks, making sure the whole does not curdle.
4 Pour into a bowl and add the juice of one large or two small lemons.
5 Stir occasionally until cool and beginning to set.
6 Stir in the whites of the eggs, which have been beaten to a stiff froth.
7 Add half a teaspoon of vanilla.
8 Chill until set, then served.

It is an improvement if thinly peeled lemon rind is added when the milk is boiled, then removed.

ANGEL FOOD FUDGE

Angel Food Fudge:

1 gill honey
1 gill water
2 whites of egg
2 cups sugar
¾ cup blanched chopped almonds
2 teaspoons orange flower water
pinch of cream of tartar

1 Dissolve the honey and sugar in the water.
2 Add cream of tartar and boil until mixture registers 123.3°C on a candy thermometer or when it forms a hard ball in the cold water test.
3 Beat egg whites stiffly.
4 Pour in the syrup gradually, beating all the time and continue beating until the mixture is stiff.
5 Add the orange flower water and the almonds.
6 Pour into a buttered tin.
7 When sufficiently cool, mark into squares.

DR CHASE'S NEW ANGEL FOOD

Whites of eleven eggs; one and a half tumblers of granulated sugar, sifted before measuring, then sifted again four times; one tumbler of plain flour measured after sifting, then sifted four times with one teaspoon of cream of tartar; then sift the flour and sugar together, with one teaspoon of vanilla. Add sugar and flour to the eggs carefully, stirring as little as possible, having previously beaten the eggs to a high froth on a large platter. Put in a pan that has never been greased and bake slowly for forty minutes. Try with a straw and if too soft let remain a few minutes longer, then turn pan upside down over a napkin on a table to cool. Then frost.

Note: A tumblerful should be considered as a large glassful.

Dr Chase's Recipe:
11 eggs
1½ tumblers sugar
1 tumbler plain flour
1 teaspoon cream of tartar
1 teaspoon vanilla

Anzac Biscuits

Question I've often wondered how Anzac biscuits got that name. Does someone know?

Answer One possible explanation for the derivation of the name is that an Anzac wafer was used during World War I by the AIF as a replacement for bread. The Anzac wafer was revived during the Second World War and the name may have been applied to the biscuit as we know it today.

FLO'S ANZAC PEANUT BISCUITS

1 Mix the first six ingredients together.
2 Heat the golden syrup, butter and bicarb soda.
3 Stir into the dry ingredients with the egg until well incorporated.
4 Knead the mixture.
5 Pinch off in small pieces, roll into balls and place on a buttered baking tray, leaving enough room for spreading.
6 Cook in the centre of a 180°C oven for 15 to 20 minutes, or until golden.
7 Remove while still warm and leave to cool and harden on a wire rack and store in an airtight container.

Flo's Anzacs
1½ cups rolled oats
1 cup SR flour
1 cup sugar
1 cup coconut
½ cup chopped peanuts
pinch salt
2 teaspoons golden syrup
115 g butter
2 teaspoons bicarb soda
1 egg

ANZAC CAKE

Anzac Cake:

115 g butter
2 cups plain flour
1 level teaspoon baking powder
1 egg
¾ cup sugar

Lemon Filling:

1 tablespoon butter
juice and zest two lemons
1 small cup sugar
1 egg

1 Cream the butter and sugar, then add the egg, flour and baking powder.
2 Place half the mixture in a tin, then spread with lemon filling (see below) and top with the other half of the mixture.
3 Decorate the top at intervals with peeled almonds.
4 Bake the cake in a moderate (180°C) oven for about twenty minutes.

Lemon Filling:

Cook all ingredients in a small saucepan until thick.

Note: The filling may be doubled if desired.

Honeycomb

Question Many years ago, at church and school fetes, we used to buy a kind of toffee known as honeycomb. How is it made?
Answer It is simple to make.

HONEYCOMB ONE

Honeycomb One:

230 g sugar
1 teaspoon bicarb soda
30 g maize syrup
1 teaspoon butter

1 Mix together the sugar and maize syrup and moisten with water.
2 Boil until the mixture reaches 165°C on a candy thermometer.
3 Remove from heat, stir in butter and bicarb.
4 Stir well and pour on to buttered trays.
5 When half cold, fold in two like a sandwich.
6 Cut with butter scissors before it is quite cold.

HONEYCOMB TWO

Honeycomb Two:

4 tablespoons sugar
2 tablespoons golden syrup
1 teaspoon bicarb soda

1 Boil sugar and syrup for seven minutes.
2 Remove from heat and add soda.
3 Mix well and pour into a buttered dish.

You would be wise to use a large saucepan as the mixture will fill two large soup plates.

Plum Pudding

Question I need a recipe for a plum pudding I can enter in the local Show. I've entered competitions before and I have been complimented on my puddings, but I still haven't won any prizes. The rules are very strict in cake and pudding competitions. Does anyone have a prize–winning recipe?

Answer Granny's prize-winning recipe has been handed down over several generations and is now passed on to Q&A. We have left it in its original imperial measures.

1 Mix dry ingredients thoroughly on kitchen paper.
2 Beat eggs well and strain.
3 Add brandy to eggs and mix well.
4 In a large bowl, mix egg-brandy mixture with the dry ingredients.
5 Grease a large basin and line it with greased waxpaper.
6 Fill basin with pudding mixture.
7 Cover basin with greased paper which has a pleat in the centre to allow rising room.
8 Cover paper with unbleached calico or similar cloth, also pleated, and tie firmly around the basin with string.
9 Secure into this, on opposite sides, three strings to form a handle.
10 Stand basin on a rack in a large saucepan with a firm fitting lid.
11 Add boiling water to reach half to two-thirds the way up the sides of the basin.
12 Boil for six hours, adding boiling water as required to maintain the level.
13 Re-boil on day of use for two hours, replacing the top cloth with a clean one. The pudding can be stored in the refrigerator between times. Serve with hard sauce or brandy-cream.

An added touch ... soak the dried fruit overnight in half a cup of rum. The rum will be enhanced by soaking four vanilla beans in the bottle of liquor for about a year. The message is—plan ahead.

Plum Pudding:
1 lb raisins
1 lb currants
1 lb prepared suet
¾ lb stale breadcrumbs
¼ lb plain flour
¼ lb brown sugar
½ lb candied peel
grated rind of 1 lemon
½ nutmeg, grated
½ pint brandy
5 eggs

Auntie's and Other Puddings

Auntie's Pudding:
raisins
currants
chopped dried apricots
breadcrumbs
1 pint warm milk
1 tablespoon sugar
1 tablespoon butter
1 tablespoon grated lemon rind
2 or 3 eggs

Butter a pudding mould and line it with raisins, currants and chopped dried apricots. (Be patriotic and use Australian dried fruits.) Make a mixture of breadcrumbs, enough to absorb one pint of warm milk. When soaked, add one tablespoon each of sugar, butter and grated lemon rind. Beat in two or three eggs. Pour the mixture into the prepared mould, cover with greased paper and steam for three hours.

MOTHER EVE'S PUDDING

Taken from Mrs Mitchell's Recipes, 1872
—now in the Mitchell Library, Sydney

'If you'd have a good pudding pray mind what
   you're taught.
Take two pennyworth of eggs when they're twelve
   for a groat*.
Take some of the same fruit with which Eve did
   once cozen,
Well pared and well chopped at least half a dozen,
Three ounces of bread, let your maid eat the crust,
The crumbs must be grated as small as the dust.
Three ounces of currants from the stones you must
   sort
Lest they break out your teeth and spoil all your
   sport.
Three ounces of sugar'll not make it too sweet
Some salt and some nutmeg to make it compleat.
Three hours let it boil without any flutter
Nor is it so good without sugar and butter.'

*A groat was a silver fourpenny piece, so two pennyworth would be six eggs.

from 'A Taste of Australia In Food and Pictures' by Peter Taylor

Bondi Pudding:
¼ lb each of flour, suet, currants, raisins and breadcrumbs
½ cup treacle
1 cup milk
essence of lemon to taste

BONDI PUDDING

1 Mix all the ingredients together well.
2 Boil for three to four hours.

GOLDEN LEMON PUFFS

1 Beat together the egg yolks and the sugar until thick and fluffy.
2 Stir in the sifted flour and the grated rind of lemon.
3 Beat the egg whites until stiff but not dry and fold into the batter.
4 Drop the batter by teaspoon into deep hot fat and fry a few at a time.
5 Drain on absorbent paper and serve with hot apricot sauce.

Golden Lemon Puffs:

4 egg yolks
10 tablespoons sugar
1½ cups sifted plain flour
grated rind two large lemons
4 egg whites

HOT APRICOT SAUCE

Wash 230 g dried apricots and soak in a saucepan of water (enough to cover) for several hours, then simmer until the fruit is soft.

Drain and puree in a blender. Add half a cup of sugar and cook over low heat, stirring until the sugar is dissolved. Add four tablespoons of brandy and serve hot.

Hot Apricot Sauce:

230 g dried apricots
water
½ cup sugar
4 tablespoons brandy

APPLE BLOSSOM PIE

1 Peel, core and slice the apples and place in a saucepan with the water and sugar.
2 Simmer until the fruit is soft.
3 Drain off the syrup and reserve for use later.
4 Add the passionfruit pulp.
5 Cool the mixture, then place in pastry case.
6 Combine the condensed milk with the egg yolk and lemon juice.
7 Beat until well mixed and spread over apple layer.
8 Dissolve the gelatine in the hot fruit syrup and add the lemon essence.
9 Set aside to cool and partly set.
10 Add a pinch of salt to the egg white and beat at high speed until stiff, then colour a pale pink with cochineal.
11 At same speed, gradually add the partly set apple syrup and continue to beat until thick.
12 Pile onto pie and decorate with whipped cream if desired.

Apple Blossom Pie:

1 cooked and cooled 23 cm pastry case
2 or 3 apples
½ cup water
¼ cup sugar
2 passionfruit
½ can sweetened condensed milk
juice of one lemon
yolk of one egg
1 level dessertspoon gelatine
1 egg white
½ teaspoon lemon essence
cochineal

Bondi Pudding

MELBOURNE BREAD AND BUTTER PUDDING

1 Either stale or freshly cut bread and butter can be used. It should be divided into conveniently sized pieces. Half of these should be placed in a pie dish and sprinkled with sugar and sultanas.
2 Beat the eggs, mix them with the milk and add a few drops of flavouring, ratafia or vanilla.
3 Pour some of the egg/milk mixture over the bread and butter in the pie dish, then add the remainder of the buttered slices and the rest of the egg and milk.
4 Leave to soak for an hour or so, then bake in a moderately hot oven until set, being careful not to let the pudding boil.

Bread and Butter Pudding:

4 or 5 slices of brown or white bread and butter
ratafia flavouring
60 g sultanas
2 eggs
570 ml milk
1½ tablespoons sugar

YARRA YARRA PIE

1 Line a pie dish with the pastry. Prick the bottom with a fork and brush lightly with beaten egg white.
2 Bake in a moderately hot oven till crisp and pale brown.
3 Break eggs into a basin and beat lightly with sugar and salt.
4 Heat the milk until tepid and stir into the egg mixture, beating constantly.
5 Fold in the coconut.
6 Pour into the baked pastry shell and bake in a slow (150°C) oven for 30 minutes.
7 Leave till cold then spread with the beaten sweetened whipped cream and sprinkle with freshly grated coconut.

from 'The New Standard Cookery Book' edited by Elizabeth Craig Odhams Press Ltd London WC2 (Attempts to trace any copyright holder have been made without success.)

Yarra Yarra Pie:

1 cup freshly grated coconut
3 eggs
2 cups milk
1 cup whipped cream
230 g shortcrust pastry
1 egg white
½ cup caster sugar
pinch of salt

VICTORIA CURRANT AND LEMON PUDDING

1 Mix all the ingredients together.
2 Put them in a greased basin and cover with greased paper.
3 Steam for two hours.

from 'The New Standard Cookery Book', edited by Elizabeth Craig Odhams Press Ltd London WC2 (Attempts to trace any copyright holder have been made without success.)

Currant and Lemon Pudding:

100 g suet
1 egg
100 g breadcrumbs
60 g flour
180 g currants
120 g sugar
rind and juice of one lemon

STEAMED PASSIONFRUIT PUDDING

Steamed Passionfruit Pudding:

suet based pastry crust
90 g caster sugar
4 tart apples
6 passionfruit

1 Line a buttered pudding basin with a thin suet crust.
2 Peel, core and slice the apples into another basin.
3 Add the pulp of the passionfruit and the sugar.
4 Mix and transfer the fruit and sugar to the lined basin.
5 Cover with a suet crust and then with a pudding cloth.
6 Steam for three hours.
7 Serve with cream.

from 'The New Standard Cookery Book', edited by Elizabeth Craig Odhams Press Ltd London WC2 (Attempts to trace any copyright holder have been made without success.)

BRISBANE CURRANT AND HONEY TART

Currant and Honey Tart:

60 g currants
2 tablespoons honey
2 tablespoons breadcrumbs
a squeeze of lemon juice
200 g short crust pastry

1 Roll out short crust pastry and line a pie plate. Cut the edges neatly and roll out the trimmings into long, narrow strips.
2 Put the honey into a saucepan with the lemon juice and warm it enough to just make it liquid.
3 Add the breadcrumbs and currants and fill the tart with this mixture.
4 Make a lattice top by twisting the pastry trimmings and laying them on the tart, pressing the ends into place.
5 Bake in a hot (220°C) oven for about 20 minutes.

from 'The New Standard Cookery Book', edited by Elizabeth Craig Odhams Press Ltd London WC2 (Attempts to trace any copyright holder have been made without success.)

Melbourne Pudding:

1 cup flour
1 cup milk
1 cup raisins, currants or dates
6 oz sugar
4 oz butter or good dripping
2 teaspoons salt
2 teaspoons bicarb of soda
nutmeg or spice to taste

MELBOURNE PUDDING

1 Mix flour and butter together, then the dry ingredients, followed by the milk in which the bicarb has been dissolved.
2 Pour into a well-floured cloth.
3 Boil for five hours.

Hasty Pudding

Question When I was a child my mother used to make something she called 'Hasty Pudding', which I loved. My wife doesn't have the recipe and I'm hoping a *Q&A*er does?

Answer Many *Q&A*ers did. Here is a selection of the recipe variations they sent in.

HASTY PUDDING THE FIRST

1 Melt the butter in a saucepan and add the flour and salt.
2 Cook for three minutes without browning.
3 Add milk gradually and stir the mixture until it boils and thickens.
4 Beat the egg yolks and sugar together and add to saucepan.
5 Pour the whole lot into an ovenproof dish and bake in a moderate (180°C) oven for ten minutes.
6 Spread with jam and top with meringue which has been made with the extra sugar and the egg whites.
7 Return to oven until top is lightly browned (about five minutes).

Serves four to six

Hasty Pudding the First:

60 g butter
4 level tablespoons plain flour
½ level teaspoon salt
570 ml milk
60 g sugar
2 eggs separated
½ teaspoon vanilla
jam (apricot is ideal)
60 g sugar for meringue topping

HASTY PUDDING THE SECOND

For each cup of milk allow one tablespoon of plain flour, sugar to taste, and one or more eggs. Put milk on to boil. Mix flour, sugar and yolks of eggs very smoothly in a basin and add to the boiling milk, stirring well till it thoroughly mixes and thickens and is quite smooth.

Beat the egg whites stiffly and fold them in. Add flavouring and pour mixture into a buttered pie dish. Dot the top with a few pieces of butter and bake in a moderate oven until golden brown.

HASTY PUDDING THE THIRD

Rub together 1½ cups of self raising flour and 1 dessertspoon of butter. Add ½ cup of milk, 2 tablespoons of boiling water and mix well. Put the lot in an ungreased basin and cover with half a cup of sugar, 1 tablespoon of golden syrup or honey, 2 dessertspoons of butter and 1 cup of boiling water.

Stand basin in boiling water and steam for half an hour. Do not cover the basin.

HASTY PUDDING THE FOURTH

Hasty Pudding the Fourth:

1 cup plain flour
¾ cup sugar
1 heaped dessertspoon cocoa
2 tablespoons butter
5 dessertspoons milk
3 eggs
1 teaspoon cream of tartar
½ teaspoon soda

1 Beat all the ingredients, except the cream of tartar, for four minutes.
2 Add cream of tartar and beat for one minute more.
3 Pour into sandwich tins and bake in a moderate oven.

If light coloured cakes are needed, omit the cocoa. This mixture also makes a good steamed pudding.

HASTY PUDDING THE FIFTH

Hasty Pudding the Fifth:

570 ml milk
1½ cups flour
1 tablespoon brown sugar
1 teaspoon cinnamon
1 dessertspoon butter

Boil milk, add sifted flour and stir until thick. Pour this mixture into a pie dish and sprinkle with brown sugar, cinnamon and butter. Leave for five to ten minutes in the hot oven, then serve hot, with cream.

Banana Pudding

Nana's Banana Pudding:

8 bananas, mashed
1 cup sugar
1 cup sultanas
3 cups fresh white breadcrumbs
juice and rind of one lemon

Question From my childhood I remember a delicious pudding Mum made with bananas. I think it was a steamed pudding. I'd like the recipe.
Answer Perhaps one of these will do.

NANA'S STEAMED BANANA PUDDING

1 Mix all together.
2 Steam in basin for two hours.
Serve with hot or cold custard.

MOCK CHRISTMAS PUDDING

1 Dissolve the bicarb in the water.
2 Mix the breadcrumbs, mixed fruit, mashed banana and beaten egg together.
3 Place in a pudding basin and steam for about two and a half hours.

Mock Christmas Pudding:

1 teaspoon bicarb of soda
1 tablespoon water
1 heaped cup of breadcrumbs
1 heaped cup mixed fruit
1 small cup mashed banana
1 egg

Brandy Snaps

Question Brandy snaps are expensive to buy. My family has expensive tastes—they love brandy snaps. How difficult are they to make? If I can make them at home I may not go bankrupt.

Answer Brandy snaps are fiddly things to make—but they look good and are certainly very popular.

1 Place golden syrup, butter and brown sugar in a saucepan and heat slowly until the butter has melted. Stir occasionally.
2 Sift flour, ginger and salt into a bowl then stir in syrup/butter mixture; mix well.
3 Drop dessertspoonsful of the mixture onto greased trays. Allow room for the inevitable spreading.
4 Bake in a moderate oven for five to seven minutes, or until golden brown.
5 Remove from oven and cool for one minute.
6 While snaps are still pliable, roll them around the greased handle of a wooden spoon. Allow them to cool on the handle.
7 Just before serving, fill with whipped cream.

Brandy Snaps:

2 tablespoons golden syrup
60 g butter
⅓ cup brown sugar
½ cup plain flour
2 teaspoons ground ginger
pinch of salt

Note: It is advisable to make only two snaps at a time. If they firm up too soon, return them to the oven for a few minutes—they will soften again.
PS: Where's the brandy?

Makes six to eight brandy snaps

Malt Bread

Question I tasted some malt bread the other day and it was delicious. Is it easy to make?

Answer It is no more difficult to make than ordinary bread. The malt does have a 'softening' effect on the gluten in the flour and bread made with malt as one of the ingredients does not have a big rise.

WHOLEMEAL MALT BREAD WITH DRIED FRUIT

Wholemeal Malt Bread:

225 g wholemeal flour
5 g salt
15 g butter
50 g currants
50 g sultanas
25 g chopped candied mixed peel
25 g soft brown sugar
15 g fresh yeast
120 ml warm milk
30 ml malt extract

1 Sift flour and salt into a warm bowl.
2 Rub in the butter and add dried fruit, mixed peel and brown sugar.
3 Blend the yeast and the warm milk and add to dry ingredients.
4 Add malt extract and mix well.
5 Turn onto a floured surface and knead dough for about three minutes or until it is smooth and elastic.
6 Place in a clean greased bowl, cover with a damp cloth and leave to rise in a warm place until it has doubled in size.
7 Turn out onto a floured surface and knead for two minutes.
8 Shape into a loaf and place in a half-kilo greased loaf tin.
9 Cover and prove in a warm place until the dough rises to near the top of the tin.
10 Bake in a very hot (230°C) oven for ten minutes, then reduce heat to fairly hot (190°C) for 25 minutes or until the bread sounds hollow when tapped.
11 Turn out to cool on a wire rack.

TREACLE AND MALT BREAD

1 Blend fresh yeast in the warm water until dissolved, or dissolve a teaspoon of sugar in water then sprinkle in the dried yeast. Leave in a warm place for ten minutes until liquid is frothy.
2 Gently heat malt extract, treacle and butter until all are melted together, then cool.
3 Add the yeast liquid and malt mixture to the dry ingredients and mix to a soft dough.
4 This dough will be too sticky to knead and should be beaten either by hand with a wooden spoon or with a mixer for two to three minutes.
5 Spoon the dough into three well-greased half-kilo tins.
6 Cover and prove for at least two hours in a warm place until the mixture is about 1 cm below the top of the tins.
7 Uncover and bake in the centre of a moderately hot (200°C) oven for 35 to 40 minutes.
8 Remove from tins and glaze with sugar syrup while still hot.

Treacle and Malt Bread:

25 g fresh yeast or 3 teaspoons dried yeast
1 teaspoon caster sugar
350 ml warm water
175 g malt extract
50 g black treacle
25 g butter
675 g strong white flour*
15 g salt
100 g sultanas (optional)

*A flour with a high gluten content

Home Made Yeasts

Question Is it possible to make yeast at home?
Answer Yes.

YEAST NUMBER ONE

1 Boil hops and water together for 20 minutes or until the hops fall to the bottom of the pan.
2 Strain and allow liquid to cool.
3 Blend flour and sugar, using a little of the hop liquor.
4 Stir all together.
5 Bottle, cork and tie down well.
6 Stand in a warm place (the bottles, that is).

This yeast will be ready for use within 24 hours.

Yeast Number One:

1 small handful of hops
1 litre water
3 tablespoons flour
3 tablespoons sugar

YEAST NUMBER TWO

Yeast Number Two:

2 handsful of hops
3 small cups bran
700 g potatoes in skins
5.5 litres water
½ cup flour
½ cup sugar
2 tablespoons salt

1 Boil together the hops, bran and potatoes which have been diced, skins and all, in the water.
2 Strain when cool.
3 Add flour and sugar to the liquid.
4 Put in an open topped jar and keep in a warm place.
5 After 24 hours, during which time the liquid should have risen to a good froth on top, add the salt.

About two cups of this yeast is used for a large batch of bread. Store in refrigerator.

Traditional German Stollen

Traditional German Stollen:

90 g fresh yeast
2 cups milk
8 cups plain flour, sifted
1 teaspoon salt
1 cup sugar
250 g butter, softened and cut up
½ cup extra plain flour for kneading
sifted icing sugar
1 cup raisins
1 cup sultanas
1 cup currants
½ cup mixed peel
½ cup chopped glace cherries
½ cup slivered almonds
melted butter for glazing

1 Crumble yeast into a large bowl.
2 Heat milk to lukewarm and pour gradually into the yeast, stirring constantly to dissolve the yeast.
3 Add the sifted flour, salt, sugar, and butter
4 Work into the dough until properly blended.
5 Cover and let rise in a warm place until the dough doubles in volume.
6 Sprinkle your work surface with a little of the extra flour and knead the dough, adding the dried fruit, peel and nuts until evenly distributed.
7 Divide dough in three or six equal portions.
8 Roll each portion into an oval and then fold each lengthways, almost in half, as you would for an omelette.
9 Place on baking tray, cover and let rise for 30 minutes.
10 Bake in a hot (205°C) oven until golden and firm, about 30 minutes for large loaves and 20–25 minutes for the medium.
11 Brush lightly with melted butter while warm.
12 Sprinkle with icing sugar when they are cool.

Makes three large or six medium loaves. The recipe may be halved.

Bushman's Brownie

Question How do you make that old favourite the Bushman's Brownie? I have lost my recipe.

Answer There are several variations of the Bushman's or Shearer's Brownie. One was given in *The Worker Cookbook*, by Dame Mary Gilmore.

1 Mix together and knead thoroughly for half an hour or longer, otherwise the brownie will be piebald.
2 A better brownie can be made by the addition of a few eggs—or many if you have them.
3 Cook slowly for 1 hour and 20 minutes.

Bushman's Brownie:
3 lbs of bread dough
2 oz butter
1½ cups sugar
1½ oz spice

SECOND VARIATION

1 Sift the flour with the baking soda, cream of tartar, spice and cinnamon.
2 Rub in the dripping.
3 Add the sugar, currants and raisins
4 Mix in sufficient milk to make a dough, a little stiffer than that for a fruitcake.
5 Place in a greased tin and bake in a fairly hot oven for approximately one hour.

Second Variation:
4 cups plain flour
1 cup each of sugar, dripping, currants and raisins
1 teaspoon each of baking soda, cream of tartar, spice and cinnamon
sufficient milk to mix

THIRD VARIATION
Ma Bonham's Brownie

1 Boil sultanas, sugar, water and salt together for five minutes
2 When cool add dry ingredients
3 Pour into a large dish (a baking dish is suitable) and cook in a moderate oven for one hour.

This brownie is moist and keeps well. The brownie was a great standby, used to fill hungry mouths during hard times.

Third Variation:
2 cups sultanas
2 cups sugar (brown may be used)
2 cups boiling water
large pinch of salt

Dry Ingredients:
4 cups self-raising flour
1 teaspoon each of bicarbonate of soda, cinnamon, mixed spice and nutmeg

Brownies:

Brownies:
1 cup raisins or mixed fruit
1 teaspoon bicarb of soda
115 g butter
¾ cup sugar
1 tablespoon golden syrup
1 teaspoon vanilla
1 cup boiling water
2 eggs
1 cup plain flour
1 cup SR flour
pinch salt

BROWNIES

1 Soak raisins and bicarb soda in the boiling water.
2 Cream the butter and sugar.
3 Add the golden syrup, vanilla and the eggs.
4 Add the fruit mixture and sifted flours and salt and mix in.
5 Bake in a moderate (180°C) oven for one hour.

This brownie keeps particularly well.

Caramel With Crème

BAKED SPUDS

First boil the potatoes for five minutes, then roll them in seasoned flour before baking with the meat.

Question Most of my caramel remains in the mould when I turn out the crème. Is there a trick to its removal along with the custard?

Answer The trick, apparently, is to pour the custard into the mould while the caramel is still hot and liquid. Bake it in a hot water bath in the usual way. Do not let the caramel set before pouring in the custard. If you still have trouble, try the following. Run a knife around the top of the custard to loosen it from the mould, then set the mould over a very low heat for just a few seconds, to melt the caramel. **(Careful!)** Place the serving plate over the mould and quickly invert. If some caramel remains, try a little more heat and pour the liquid caramel over and around the custard.

The classic crème caramel, or baked caramel custard, remains a favourite with many people, although devalued by some writers in recent times.

It is a simple self-indulgence many of us enjoy. It is not difficult to make. Here are three variations—the French—the Anglaise—and the Filipino.

CREME RENVERSEE

1 Put sugar and water into a four-cup pan.
2 Heat until sugar caramelises and turns a dark brown.
3 Remove pan from heat and make sure caramel coats bottom and sides of pan.
4 Place pan in cold water to stop the caramel cooking.
5 In a separate pan add vanilla bean (or essence) to milk and bring to boil.
6 Beat eggs with a whisk.
7 Add sugar and the salt.
8 Pour half the hot milk into the egg/sugar mixture.
9 Stir and then add the rest of the hot milk.
10 Add vanilla extract at this stage if the bean has not been used.
11 Mix well and strain custard into caramel coated pan.
12 Skim foam from top of custard. If left there and baked it will become tough.
13 Set pan in a hot-water bath.
14 Bake on lowest shelf of a pre-heated 165°C oven for about 50 minutes, or until done. The test for cooked custard is to gently shake the pan. If the wiggle is a firm one, then the custard is done. A flabby wiggle means another five minutes cooking is necessary. Start testing after 40 minutes.
15 Cool on a wire rack, and refrigerate until very cold. Unmould just before serving. The custard may crack if left out of the mould for too long.

Crème Renverse:

4 tablespoons sugar
4 tablespoons water
2 cups milk
4 whole eggs
¾ cup sugar
pinch salt
1 teaspoon vanilla essence or 2 inch piece vanilla bean

LECHE FLAN

1 Caramelise pan as for first recipe.
2 Beat yolks, then add milk, both condensed and fresh and the vanilla.
3 Pour mixture into caramelised pan and place in a larger pan containing boiling water.
4 Cook for about 50 minutes or until firm, in a 165°C oven.
5 Remove from pan for serving, as in first recipe.

Leche Flan:

8 egg yolks
1 can sweetened condensed milk
equal quantity milk
2 teaspoons vanilla essence

CREME CARAMEL
The Anglaise Way

Crème Caramel:

| 2 cups milk |
| 8 egg yolks |
| 10 tablespoons sugar |
| ½ teaspoon salt |
| 6 tablespoons whipping cream |
| 1 teaspoon vanilla, or 2 inch piece vanilla bean |

1 Scald milk in saucepan. Split vanilla bean, if used, and add to milk.
2 Beat yolks in another pan.
3 Add sugar and salt and mix well.
4 Add half the hot milk, stir, then add the rest.
5 Cook sauce over low heat, and stir until it coats the back of a spoon. Do **not** boil, or the custard will curdle.
6 When custard has thickened set it immediately into cold water to stop it cooking.
7 Stir until cool.
8 Add cream and vanilla, if using extract. If the bean has been used remove it at this stage.
9 Strain custard into prepared caramelised pan (see first recipe).
10 Set pan in water bath.
11 Bake on lowest shelf of oven at 165°C for about 50 minutes. Test as for first recipe.
12 When cooked, remove and refrigerate.
13 When ready to serve, treat as for first recipe.

Caramel Sauces

Question Some time ago someone asked for a recipe for the chocolate sauce which was served at Cahill's restaurants. I'd like the recipe for their caramel sauce.

Answer We received a number of caramel sauce recipes which our correspondents claim give very similar results to the sauce served at Cahills.

CARAMEL BRANDY SAUCE

Caramel Brandy Sauce:

| ¼ cup butter |
| 1 cup brown sugar |
| ½ cup cream |
| 2 eggs |
| 1 tablespoons brandy or rum |

1 Cream the butter and stir in the sugar gradually.
2 Add the brandy or rum very slowly.
3 Add the well-beaten egg yolks and the cream.
4 Cook until thick, stirring constantly.
5 Remove from the heat and add the stiffly beaten egg whites.

This is ideal with Christmas pud.

GOLDEN SYRUP CARAMEL SAUCE

1 Melt butter, sugar, condensed milk and golden syrup over medium heat.
2 Stir with wooden spoon until mixture is a rich, deep caramel colour (about 20 minutes).
3 Remove from heat and add boiling water a little at a time, mixing in well.
4 Return to heat and boil for a few minutes. The mixture will thicken as it cools.

For a thinner sauce, use 12 tablespoons of water.

Golden Syrup Caramel Sauce:
6❸ g butter
4 tablespoons brown sugar
4 tablespoons condensed milk
2 dessertspoons golden syrup
8 tablespoons boiling water

SUPER CARAMEL SAUCE

1 Place sugar and cold water over medium heat, stirring until syrup is a clear brown, but not dark, caramel.
2 Carefully add hot water (beware of splashing).
3 Stir until well blended.
4 Add cornflour which has been mixed with a little cold water.
5 Boil for five minutes.
6 Continue the cooking over water (double boiler) for 15 minutes, stirring all the time.
7 Beat in butter and vanilla.

Super Caramel Sauce:
1 cup sugar
1 tablespoon cold water
1⅓ cups hot water
1 tablespoon cornflour
1 tablespoon butter
1 teaspoon vanilla

RICH CARAMEL SAUCE

1 Melt butter in medium sized saucepan.
2 Add sugar and glucose.
3 Stir over medium heat until sugar dissolves. Do not boil.
4 Increase heat and boil steadily for five minutes. Do not stir while boiling. It may be necessary to reduce heat during this boiling to prevent burning.
5 Remove from heat and allow bubbles to subside.
6 Gradually stir in the cream.

This will make a little over three cups of sauce.

Rich Caramel Sauce:
125 g butter
2 cups brown sugar (lightly packed)
⅔ cup liquid glucose
300 ml carton cream

Marshmallow Caramel Sauce:

125 g butter
¾ cup brown sugar, lightly packed
100 g packet white marshmallows
⅓ cup milk

MARSHMALLOW CARAMEL SAUCE

1 Melt butter in a medium sized saucepan with a heavy base.
2 Add sugar, marshmallows and milk and stir over low heat until the sugar is dissolved and the marshmallows melted. Do not allow to boil.
3 Increase the heat and boil gently without stirring for five minutes. By now the mixture should be golden.
4 Allow the sauce to stand for five minutes before serving.

This makes approximately one and a quarter cups.

Chocolate Sauces

Question Anyone living in Sydney a few years ago would remember the wonderful chocolate sauce served over ice cream at Cahill's Restaurants. But does anyone know how to make that sauce?

Answer The request for the chocolate sauce recipe brought to light a wide variety of recipes using chocolate in its various forms.

BRANDIED CHOCOLATE SAUCE

Brandied Chocolate Sauce:

½ cup sugar
½ cup cream
1½ teaspoons butter
60 g dark chocolate
2 tablespoons brandy
½ teaspoon vanilla

1 Place half a cup of sugar and half a cup of cream, together with one and a half teaspoons of butter and 60 g of chopped dark chocolate into a saucepan.
2 Stir over low heat until butter and chocolate have melted.
3 Increase heat, stir until sauce boils.
4 Reduce heat and simmer gently without stirring for five minutes.
5 Remove from heat and add two tablespoons of brandy and half a teaspoon vanilla.

This makes about one cup of sauce. It is excellent with profiteroles.

CHOCOLATE SAUCE WITH GOLDEN SYRUP

1 Put sugar, golden syrup, one cup of water and butter in pan and boil.
2 Mix cornflour with remaining half cup of water.
3 Add this to mixture in pan together with the dry cocoa.
4 Stir well and allow to boil for two minutes.
5 Add vanilla and stir well.

HOT FUDGE SAUCE

1 Melt chocolate in milk stirring constantly. (The melting can be done in a microwave oven.)
2 Beat until smooth.
3 Add one teaspoon of salt, the sugar and the light corn syrup.
4. Return to heat and cook for five minutes, stirring.
5 Add butter and vanilla.

Serve warm or cold on ice cream, pancakes, cream puffs. This sauce keeps well in the refrigerator and can be reheated.

SIMPLE CHOCOLATE SAUCE

1 Mix chocolate and brown sugar with the cream.
2 Stir over hot water until thickened and blended.

INSTANT COFFEE CHOCOLATE SAUCE

1 In top part of double boiler mix sugar, cocoa, coffee powder, water.
2 Cover with lid and place on bottom half of boiler containing simmering water.
3 Stir at intervals for about half an hour or until the sauce reaches the desired consistency.
4 A richer sauce may be made by adding one beaten egg yolk gradually to the finished sauce.
5 Keep in refrigerator.

Chocolate Sauce with Golden Syrup:

60 g cocoa
½ teaspoon vanilla
¾ cup white sugar
1 tablespoon golden syrup
¾ tablespoon cornflour
1½ cups water
1 teaspoon butter

Hot Fudge Sauce:

375 g unsweetened chocolate
3 cups of milk
1 teaspoon salt
6 cups sugar
¾ cup light corn syrup
⅓ cup butter
1 tablespoon vanilla essence

Simple Chocolate Sauce:

½ cup of cream
125 g grated chocolate
60 g brown sugar

Instant Coffee Sauce:

¾ cup sugar
2 tablespoons cocoa
1 cup of water
½ teaspoon instant coffee powder
1 egg yolk, optional

Country Style Sauce:

1½ cups brown sugar

2 tablespoons butter

3 tablespoons cocoa

¼ cup hot water

½ cup cream

vanilla

pinch of salt

Smooth Chocolate Sauce:

¾ cup milk

120 g grated chocolate

¼ cup water

2 teaspoons plain flour

30 g unsalted butter

pinch salt

¼ teaspoon vanilla essence

Economical Sauce:

1 cup sugar

1½ cups water

½ teaspoon vanilla

2 heaped tablespoons cocoa

Velvet Chocolate Sauce:

110 g semi sweet chocolate

¾ cup sugar

pinch of salt

¾ cup undiluted evaporated milk

2 teaspoons vanilla extract

1½ teaspoons dark rum

COUNTRY STYLE CHOCOLATE SAUCE

1 Mix cocoa with butter, sugar and salt.
2 Add hot water and heat until sugar is dissolved.
3 Cook slowly for ten minutes.
4 Remove from heat and add cream.
5 Beat well and add vanilla.
6 Serve warm over ice cream.

SMOOTH CHOCOLATE SAUCE

1 Heat milk and chocolate over boiling water.
2 When chocolate melts beat until smooth.
3 Combine sugar, flour and salt and blend with a little cold milk.
4 Stir into chocolate mixture.
5 Cook for five minutes, stirring until thickened.
6 Remove from heat, add butter and vanilla and stir until smooth.

ECONOMICAL CHOCOLATE SAUCE

1 Mix cocoa, sugar and water.
2 Bring to boil and let simmer for half an hour to one hour.
3 Cool and add vanilla.
4 Stir till smooth.

VELVET CHOCOLATE SAUCE

1 Melt chocolate in top part of double boiler.
2 Stir in sugar, cover and cook over simmering water for 15 minutes, stirring occasionally.
3 Stir in remaining ingredients.
4 Cover and keep warm over water until ready to serve.

Double Cream (Crème Fraiche)

Question What are double cream and *crème fraiche?*

Answer Double cream, called for in many recipes, has a butterfat content of between 40 and 48 per cent. Single cream has a butterfat content of between 36 and 40 per cent. Cream for butter making usually tests at 38 to 42 per cent, but cream for domestic use usually has a lower butter fat content, for reasons of economy. Today, cream for domestic use is often artificially thickened.

Double cream may be made at home if you have a microwave oven. Pour two 300 ml cartons of cream into a large bowl and place it into the microwave oven. Use full power for 24 minutes, stirring every five minutes. At the end of the time, the cream will be reduced and quite thick. Its butterfat content will have effectively doubled.

Crème Fraiche is a thick, sweet-sour cream much used in French cooking. It is freely available in Europe and now is available commercially in Australia. However, it can be made at home. It is a valuable addition to many recipes.

WHIPPED CREAM

Use honey instead of sugar when whipping cream. It will stay firmer and keep longer.

CREME FRAICHE

1 Pour 300 ml of cream into a jar.
2 Add three tablespoons of commercial plain yoghurt, or buttermilk.
3 Mix well and place in a warm spot for about eight hours, or overnight. If your oven has a pilot light, this is ideal. A domestic yoghurt maker is also suitable. Otherwise stand the jar in a bowl of water at blood heat. Keep the water close to this temperature for about eight hours.
4 Next morning, stir and refrigerate. The *crème fraiche* will thicken as it gets cold.
5 When down to your last two or three tablespoons of *crème fraiche*, use it as a starter for your next batch.

Clotted Cream

Question How does one make the clotted cream I remember from those wonderful Devonshire teas—freshly made scones and home-made jam topped with clotted cream? There are few pleasures in the world to equal a good Devonshire tea!

Answer 'Clowtyd crayme and nawe crayme out together, is eaten more for a sensuall appetyte than for any good nourishment.' (Boorde)

Clotted cream is still a speciality of the English counties, Devon and Cornwall. Dispute exists over the origin of the name. A 'clout' is a thick patch, possibly of leather. Clotted cream wrinkles into thick, leathery folds. The old spellings include clowtyd, clouted, clowted, clawted and clotted.

In early days the cream was probably the thick, wrinkled, folded, yellow, crusted cream as made by the folk of Cornwall and Devon to this day. These instructions originate in East Ogwell, Devon, from very early this century.

'Set very fresh milk to stand in a wide earthenware pan with handles, for twelve hours in summer or twenty four hours in winter. Heat slowly, never allowing to boil, until the shape of the bottom of the pan is outlined in the cream, as a circle concentric to the rim of the pan. Without disturbing the pan, remove from the heat and leave to cool for a further twelve hours in a cool place. The thick crust of cream is then skimmed off with a large spoon or slice. The top will be golden yellow and very creamy underneath.'

This cream is used in many ways in both Devon and Cornwall: a little spread on buns, called splits; poured into pork and leek pies; in Lammy pie, which is lamb, layered with lots of chopped parsley and cream, with pastry over the top.

Clotting the quick way: Use a double boiler, or stand a pan of cream in a saucepan of water (a bain marie). With a thermometer check when the cream reaches a temperature of around 76–82°C. Keep the cream at around this temperature for up to one hour, until the cream looks crusty and wrinkled. Early in the proceedings stir the cream once, to distribute the heat. Cool the cream pan quickly, by standing it in a pan of cold water, then leave it in a cool place overnight to set. Pack the clotted cream, which you have skimmed from the bowl, in jars and store in the refrigerator.

Note: Do not attempt to make clotted cream from homogenised milk. It just will not happen.

'. . . My landlady brought me one of the west country tarts . . . it is an apple pie with custard all on top. It is the most acceptable entertainment that could be made me. They scald their cream and milk in most parts of these counties and so it is a sort of clouted cream as we call it, with a little sugar, and so put on top of the apple pie.'

Through England On a Side-Saddle, Celia Fiennes, 1662–1741

Royal Icing

Question I'm having trouble getting my royal icing to set in the warmer weather. What should I do?

Answer Royal icing contains egg white and lemon juice (acetic acid) and **always** pure icing sugar.

Put 1 kg of pure icing sugar into a bowl and add egg whites one at a time. The egg whites should not be whisked, only beaten a little to break them. Care should be taken to ensure that **no** egg yolk goes in with the white. Use as few whites as possible—three will probably be sufficient for 1 kg of icing sugar. As the first egg white is worked into the sugar add a few drops of lemon juice now and then. When it has been worked for a while add another egg white and a little more lemon juice. The royal icing may be tested by placing a little on a piece of dry bread. If it does not run, it is ready.

Additional acetic acid (available from the chemist) may be added if you have setting problems with the royal icing.

Royal Icing:

1 kg pure icing sugar
3 egg whites
few drops lemon juice
acetic acid

Marshmallow Frosting

Question I have a youngster's birthday party approaching and I have promised to provide the cake. I would like to decorate it with marshmallow icing but do not have the recipe.

Answer Three versions follow:

FROSTING ONE

Frosting One:

1 cup sugar
1 cup water
1 tablespoon gelatine
¼ teaspoon vanilla
colouring

1 Boil all ingredients together for five minutes at 110°C.
2 Cool.
3 Beat until peaks form.
4 Spread on cake. Dip knife in hot water if the frosting is sticky. It is advisable to have the decorations handy as this frosting sets very quickly. Use marshmallows as 'bubbles' to hold the candles. Cutting the cake will be easier if the knife is dipped in hot water.

FROSTING TWO

Frosting Two:

2 egg whites
2¼ cups granulated sugar
4 tablespoons cold water
9 large marshmallows, cut small
½ teaspoon vanilla
¼ teaspoon baking powder

1 Place egg whites, sugar and water in the top of a double boiler.
2 Place over boiling water.
3 Beat with egg beater for about ten minutes, until thick.
4 Add the marshmallow pieces as the mixture thickens and beat until smooth.
5 Remove from the heat and add flavouring.
6 Continue to beat and add baking powder.
7 When thick, spread on cake.

FROSTING THREE

Frosting Three:

1¼ cups sugar
½ cup water
3 egg whites

1 Combine sugar and water in a small saucepan.
2 Stir over medium heat until sugar is dissolved. Do not boil.
3 Push any grains of sugar down from sides of pan with brush which has been dipped in water.
4 Increase heat and boil rapidly, uncovered, for three to five minutes. Do not stir after syrup boils. Syrup should reach 115°C on syrup

thermometer. If one is not available, test by dropping one teaspoon of syrup into cold water. At the right temperature it will form a soft, sticky toffee ball when rolled between the fingers. The syrup should not change colour. If it does, you have gone too far and will have to start again.

5 While the syrup boils, beat egg whites until stiff in a small bowl with an electric beater. Keep beating while syrup reaches right temperature.

6 When syrup is ready, allow bubbles to subside, then pour in a thin stream on to the egg whites while they are being beaten on medium speed. Do not add syrup too quickly or the frosting will not thicken.

7 Continue beating and adding syrup until all syrup is used.

8 Continue to beat until frosting stands in stiff peaks.

9 Colour if desired, at this stage, by folding colouring through with beater on low speed, or with a wooden spoon.

10 Spread over cake. For best results this should be done the day the cake is to be served, when the frosting is fresh and has a marshmallow consistency.

Mock Almond Paste

Question I'm very fond of almond paste on cakes and I've often wondered whether it is possible to make it at home?

Answer An almond paste substitute is relatively easy to make. Here's one from a very old cookbook.

1 Sift the icing sugar and add the coconut.

2 Mix to a stiff paste with the sherry, egg yolk and essence.

3 On a board dusted with icing sugar roll out the paste to the desired size.

4 Cover the cake.

If two egg yolks are used, the almond paste is less likely to topple off the cake when it is cut.

Mock Almond Paste:

½ **lb icing sugar**
½ **lb dessicated coconut**
yolk of one egg
1 teaspoon almond essence
1 tablespoon sherry

MOCK ALMOND PASTE 2

Mock Almond Paste 2:

680 g icing sugar
230 g almond meal or marzipan
3 egg yolks
juice of ½ lemon
1 tablespoon of glycerine
a little sherry

1 Sift the sugar and almond meal and mix well.
2 Add egg yolks, lemon juice and glycerine.
3 Mix into a stiff dough with a little sherry.
4 Turn onto a pastry board, which has been sprinkled with icing sugar and knead lightly, then roll to shape.

This quantity will cover a small cake. Double the quantities for a 25 cm cake. Before placing almond paste on the cake, brush the cake well with egg white to stop the paste moving.

Mock Maple Syrup

Question I've been told it is possible to make mock maple syrup. Is this so?

Answer Mock maple syrup usually contains honey, golden syrup or brown sugar. The following recipes may be worth trying.

MOCK MAPLE ONE

Mock Maple One:

2 tablespoons honey
1 tablespoon golden syrup
1 tablespoon boiling water
1 teaspoon lemon juice

1 Mix the honey, golden syrup and boiling water together.
2 Add the lemon juice and stir well.
3 Warm slightly by placing in a double boiler for a few minutes.

Serve with waffles or fruit fritters.

MOCK MAPLE TWO

Mix together equal quantities of honey, golden syrup and boiling water. Stir in vanilla essence and a sprinkling of cinnamon.

MOCK MAPLE THREE

Mock Maple Three:

1 cup light brown sugar
⅓ cup water
pinch of salt
¼ teaspoon vanilla

1 Dissolve the sugar in the water.
2 Add the salt and boil for one minute.
3 Add vanilla and mix.

Serve hot or cold.

Preserving Olives

Question I'm one of those people who like to do their own thing, and that extends to preserving my own olives. However, I haven't had much success—the olives usually grow a fungus before they're properly preserved. Where am I going wrong?

Answer Even ripe olives are too bitter to be eaten as they stand. It is necessary to pickle them before they are truly edible. The process is quite involved, particularly for unripe and green olives and it is probably easier to buy your own olives, already preserved. However, those who prefer to 'do their own thing' may like to try the following methods.

> ## CAULIFLOWER
> A small quantity of milk, or a pinch of baking powder, added to the cooking water will keep cauliflower white.

BLACK OLIVES

1 Take ripe, black olives and soak them in several changes of water for about 24 hours, to remove their bitterness.
2 Drain the water from the olives and place them in suitable, sealable jars.
3 Fill the jars with a brine made from pickling salt and water—about 100 g of salt to each litre of water.
4 Make sure the jars are full of olives and brine, seal and leave for at least four months.

GREEN OLIVES

1 Unripe green olives should be split before they are placed in water for leaching.
2 Change the water every day for about ten days.
3 Make a brine by boiling about 100 g salt to each litre of water, together with a bay leaf, a little garlic and some fennel. Chilli may also be added, if desired.
4 Make sure the brine solution is cold before pouring it over the split green olives. Use suitable sealable jars and make sure the brine covers the olives completely.
5 Leave for three to four months.

Preserving Olives

Garlic is a-peeling

Question What's the best way to peel garlic?
Answer There are as many ways to peel garlic as
there are cooks. Each budding Dumas has his/her
own highly successful method of divesting the
aromatic, alliaceous Asian plant of its indigestible
epidermis—thus giving access to one of the most
wonderful flavouring agents God has given the
human race. That race, of course, is divided into
two opposing camps: those who eat garlic and those
who don't—and never the twain shall meet.

They may be united, however, in their admiration
for the qualities of this cousin of the onion. It is a
matter of record that the slaves who built the Great
Pyramids of Egypt were given a daily ration of
garlic to keep them strong enough to carry out their
arduous tasks. On the day the ration failed to
appear, the slaves downed their tools in protest.

Garlic is also a renowned medicinal herb. An old
Spanish proverb says: 'Where you find garlic you
find good health'. At the baptism of King Henri IV
of France a clove of garlic was rubbed on his
tongue. This was followed by a sip of armagnac. To
this day, some French parents continue the practice.

But to business... One can crush the clove with
the skin attached. Usually, the outer skin is then
removed quite easily. The flat of a broad knife and
a little salt together make using garlic quite easy.
Put the cloves of garlic, together with the salt, in a
pile on your cutting board. Attack them with the
broadside of the blade. The salt softens the bulb,
combines with the juice, and the skin separates.

It is said that a new recipe should never be tried on
guests. This is a rule one should certainly apply to
a recipe containing thirty cloves of garlic. I broke
the rule, and with great success. The guests
demanded the recipe, which my sister, Mary
McCormack, had foisted on me. It is one of those
recipes that call for the garlic clove whole—skin and
all—in what may seem excessive amounts.

ROOT GINGER

To prevent root ginger
from drying out first
peel and cut into
pieces. Then store in
a jar of dry sherry, in
the refrigerator. The
ginger will keep
indefinitely. The
sherry is also useful
in Chinese cooking.
Top up the jar when
necessary.

CHICKEN WITH GARLIC (LOTS)

Chicken With Garlic:

1 chicken
40 g butter
4 tablespoons olive oil
30 cloves of garlic
10 shallots
dry white wine

1 Cut chicken into eight pieces.
2 Melt butter in casserole, add oil and heat until smoking.
3 Brown chicken pieces all over on a moderate heat. Make sure the oil and butter do not burn.
4 Put the garlic cloves—**unpeeled**—and the shallots, which have been chopped finely, in with the chicken.
5 Simmer for ten minutes.
6 Add a glass of white wine, plenty of white pepper, and a little salt, if desired.
7 Place the lid on the casserole and simmer for 30 minutes.
8 Remove the lid and raise the heat to evaporate the wine completely and brown the chicken again.
9 Remove chicken from the casserole to a warmed platter.
10 Serve the garlic cloves with the chicken.

Do not hesitate! A mouthful of chicken, followed by a clove of garlic! Heaven! Spit out the garlic skin discreetly. Sip dry white wine.

Without doubt, this is the best method I know of removing the skins from cloves of garlic. Thank you, Mary!

Chokos

Question My neighbour's choko vine is trailing over my fence. It's loaded with fruit and I'd like to take advantage of those on my property. How does one prepare chokos for eating?

Answer Choko is the name used in Australia for the *chayote*, a member of the gourd family indigenous to Mexico, the West Indies and Central America. In the United States it is known variously as mirliton, mango squash, vegetable pear, pepinella, brionne and custard marrow. When preparing chokos it is best to peel them under running water. Rubber gloves should be worn to protect the hands. The fruit should be halved and the seeds removed. If the fruit is large it should be cut into quarters.

CHOKO (OR MOCK-APPLE) PIE

1 Peel and thinly slice the chokos.
2 Place in pan with two cups of water and cook until tender. Drain and mash.
3 Return to pan, add sugar and tartaric acid *OR* lemon juice, then add cornflour *OR* custard powder, which has been made into a paste with a small amount of water.
4 Add two cloves and cook the lot until thick.
5 Use as a pie filling.

Chokos can be used as a superb strudel filling—but don't tell anyone until after their first bite.

1 Peel, halve, and remove the seeds from three or four chokos.
2 Place in pan and cover with water.
3 Add two cloves, sugar to taste and juice of one lemon.
4 Cook until tender.
5 Drain and refrigerate.
6 When you wish to prepare the strudel, add a few crushed walnuts, a handful or two of breadcrumbs, and a little arrowroot to thicken, if necessary. Spread this mixture over a square of commercial puff pastry, roll up and bake until golden brown.

Serve either hot or cold, with whipped cream.

Choko Pie:

3 medium or 4 small chokos
1 teaspoon tartaric acid or juice of 2 lemons
¾ cup sugar
2½ tablespoons cornflour or custard powder
cloves

FRIED CHOKO RINGS

Peel chokos and cut into slices 1 cm thick. Throw into boiling salted water and cook for 15 minutes. Drain well and remove the centre seeds. Dip the choko rings in seasoned flour, then in beaten egg and then in sieved stale breadcrumbs. Fry in deep smoking hot fat until brown and crisp. Drain on kitchen paper and sprinkle with grated cheese. These choko rings are excellent served with mixed grills, including bacon.

Fried Choko Rings:

chokos
water
salt
seasoned flour
beaten egg
stale bread crumbs
fat for frying
grated cheese

from 'The New Standard Cookery Book', edited by Elizabeth Craig Odhams Press Ltd London WC2 (Attempts to trace any copyright holder have been made without success.)

Coping With Cumquats

Question I think a lot of people have the same problem I have—what to do with an overabundance of cumquats. Recipes to use them up would be most welcome.

Answer A number of listeners called in and wrote with suggestions as to what our caller could do with his cumquats. The suggestions included recipes for cumquat liquer, preserved cumquats, crystallised cumquats, glace cumquats, cumquat marmalade and cumquat jelly.

CUMQUAT LIQUEUR

Cumquat Liqueur:

15 large cumquats or 30 small cumquats
1 bottle of gin
500 g loaf sugar

1 Prick the cumquats all over with a darning needle.
2 Put them all in a large screw-top jar.
3 Pour in the gin (the whole bottle, mind you!).
4 Add the loaf sugar. It must be loaf sugar.
5 Keep in a cool place for at least three months.
6 At the end of this minimum period, when the fruit has had time to become impregnated with the sweetened gin, pour off the liquer.
7 Store the liquer in a suitable decanter.
8 The fruit should not be wasted. Cut the cumquats into small segments, dry on paper towel and roll in sugar. These segments may be served with coffee, together with the liqueur.

Inexpensive brandy may be substituted for the gin in this recipe.

ALTERNATIVE LIQUEUR

Alternative Liqueur:

20 cumquats
450 g sugar
1 stick cinnamon
1 bottle brandy, gin or vodka

1 Prick cumquats with a sharp needle.
2 Layer in large mouthed jar with sugar.
3 Let stand overnight.
4 Cover with the liquor and add cinnamon stick.
5 Seal.
6 Hide in cupboard for about six months.

GLACE CUMQUATS

1 Using a fine needle, make no more than eight pricks in the skin of each cumquat.
2 Cover the fruit with cold water to which has been added one tablespoon of salt.
3 Soak overnight and then drain.
4 Put the cumquats into a pan with fresh cold water to cover.
5 Bring to the boil and simmer until tender, about 30 minutes. then drain.
6 Place the cumquats in syrup to cover. The syrup is made from 500 g of sugar to each two and a half cups of water.
7 Cook until clear and transparent.
8 Place in a bowl and allow to stand overnight.
9 Drain the syrup into a saucepan.
10 Add an extra quarter cup of sugar.
11 Bring to the boil and pour over cumquats.
12 Leave for 48 hours.
13 Repeat this process once more, adding the extra quarter cup of sugar as before, and leaving the whole lot to stand for a further 48 hours.
14 Drain the syrup from the fruit.
15 Roll the cumquats in coarse sugar and dry in the sun or in a very slow oven.

Glacé Cumquats:

cumquats
water
salt
sugar

CUMQUAT CONSERVE

1 Take six dozen cumquats, with stems, and leave for three days, till the stems rub off without leaving a hole. (A hole would allow liquid to enter the fruit and spoil it.)
2 Put cumquats in a preserving pan and just cover with cold water.
3 Add one cup of salt.
4 Boil gently for half an hour.
5 Strain off water.
6 Cover with water and add bicarb soda.
7 Bring to the boil for 20 minutes and strain again.
8 Prick the fruit all over and then weigh.
9 Make a syrup of 450 g of sugar and one cup of water to every 450 g of fruit.
10 Boil the whole lot for three hours or until the syrup is very thick.
11 Bottle while hot in sterilised jars and seal.

Cumquat Conserve:

6 doz cumquats
water
1 cup salt
1 teaspoon bicarb soda
sugar

CUMQUAT AND CARROT MARMALADE

Cumquat and Carrot Marmalade:

½ kg cumquats

½ kg carrots

sugar

small knob of butter

1 Cut cumquats in half and remove pips, which should be soaked in a little hot water (for the pectin).
2 Slice the cumquats finely.
3 Peel and grate the carrots and place them in a bowl. Cover with water and allow to soak overnight.
4 The following day put the fruit and the water from the cumquat pips in a preserving pan and simmer until tender. This should take about half an hour.
5 Measure the fruit and add one cup of sugar to one generous cup of the fruit.
6 Add the butter and return to heat.
7 When the sugar has dissolved, boil rapidly until the setting point is reached.
8 Remove marmalade from heat and let stand for five minutes.
9 Stir, then put in sterilised jars and seal while it is still hot.

CUMQUAT MARMALADE WITHOUT SEEDS

Seedless Cumquat Marmalade:

1.5 kg cumquats

2.5 kg sugar

3.5 litres water

juice two lemons

1 Wash fruit.
2 Slice finely and put seeds aside in a small basin.
3 Place fruit in a large saucepan and cover with three litres of water.
4 Cover seeds with remaining half litre of water and leave overnight.
5 The next day, boil fruit and liquid with the strained liquid from the seeds, until rind is tender and liquid is reduced by half.
6 Add sugar and lemon juice.
7 Stir over low heat until sugar is dissolved.
8 Boil rapidly for approximately one and a half hours, or until marmalade jells when tested on a cold saucer.
9 Pour into hot, sterilised jars and seal.

This makes about 2.5 litres of marmalade.

CUMQUAT JELLY

1 Soak cumquats for 24 hours in salt and water (about one cup of salt to five litres of water).
2 Pour off water and slice or quarter fruit.
3 Add one lemon (cut up) for every dozen cumquats.
4 Place fruit in preserving pan with enough water to float it.
5 Boil for two hours, or until fruit is quite tender.
6 Strain, without squeezing, through a jelly bag.
7 Add one cup of sugar to each cup of juice.
8 Boil for about half an hour, or until it 'jells'.
9 Do not stir jelly after sugar is melted.
10 Pour into jars while hot, and seal.

Cumquat Jelly:

cumquats

salt

water

lemons

sugar

CRYSTALLISED CUMQUATS

1 Select nice firm fruit and cook for a short period in clear water.
2 Use sufficient of this water to make a syrup, allowing 725 g of sugar to each 450 g of fruit and liquid.
3 Put the cumquats into the hot syrup.
4 Stand for two days.
5 Drain off the syrup and boil again until it thickens.
6 Return the cumquats to the thickened syrup.
7 Repeat the process until the syrup no longer goes thin after boiling.
8 Dry cumquats in the sun or a very slow oven.
9 Roll them in granulated sugar, then bottle.

These crystallised cumquats are particularly good after dinner and can be made even better by dipping them in chocolate.

PRESERVED CUMQUATS OR MANDARINS

1 Prick the fruit with a sharp needle.
2 Boil gently in plenty of water, until tender.
3 Make a syrup with 500 g of sugar and 300 ml of water to each dozen fruit.
4 Boil this syrup for 20 minutes.
5 Add fruit and simmer for five minutes more.
6 Bottle hot.

Quite a Caper

Question How does one make capers? Also, is it true that capers are actually preserved nasturtium seeds?

Answer Capers are not nasturtium seeds. They come from the caper plant, a spiny Mediterranean shrub, *Capparis spinosa*, which also grows in the East Indies and the orient. Capers are the unopened flower buds of the shrub, although they do resemble nasturtium seeds. Nasturtium seeds can also be pickled successfully.

Capers have been used as a condiment for at least 2000 years. Capric acid, which develops when the buds are pickled, is responsible for the characteristic flavour. In England they are used to flavour the sauce which is the traditional accompaniment to boiled mutton. They are also used in antipasto or added to mayonnaise or salad dressings. Good capers are olive green in colour. They are firm and have a piece of stalk still attached. The best capers are from the French areas of Var and Bouches-de-Rhone and are known as 'none-such' capers.

PICKLED CAPERS
Capperi Sott'aceto

1 Sprinkle capers generously with salt and leave for several hours.
2 Cover with vinegar and let stand for one day longer.
3 Drain and place capers in bottles.
4 Cover with fresh vinegar which has been boiled and then cooled.
5 Alternatively, put capers in a brine made with 60 g of kitchen salt to each 600 ml of water.
6 Leave for 24 hours.
7 Drain, but do not wash.
8 Put capers in jars and pour over hot vinegar.
9 Cover, seal and store.
10 To make the spiced vinegar, add one teaspoon of mixed pickling spice to each 600 ml of white vinegar and boil for 15 minutes. Strain.

Shelling Pecans

Question A simple question—what's the best way to shell pecans?

Answer This question raised another: the proper way to pronounce pecan. We were assured that the locals in pecan-growing areas of the United States pronounce the name with a long 'a'. Some authorities decree it may be pronounced with either the short or long 'a'.

The edible pecan comes from Carya pecan, a hickory tree of the southern United States.

A special pecan-sheller is available. If this is not in your collection of kitchen implements, then the nuts can be shelled relatively easily if boiling water is poured over them and they are left to stand for 15 to 20 minutes. Garden secateurs may also be used to shell the pecan quickly and effectively. Use them to nip off each end of the shell, then hold the nut lengthways along the blade of the secateurs, with the seam facing to the side. Pressure with the secateurs will split the shell. The de-shelled nuts should be stored in airtight jars.

PECAN SCROLLS

Pecan Scrolls:

½ cup butter

1 cup brown sugar

2 well beaten eggs

½ teaspoon vanilla

4 tablespoons SR flour

½ teaspoon salt

½ cup pecans

1 Cream butter.
2 Add brown sugar gradually and beat well until light.
3 Add well beaten eggs to butter/sugar mixture and blend well.
4 Add vanilla, flour and salt and mix thoroughly.
5 Add finely chopped pecans.
6 Drop scant teaspoonfuls onto a greased baking tray and with the back of a spoon spread mixture as thinly as possible. Leave about 10 cm between wafers.
7 Bake in a moderate (165°C) oven for 10 to 12 minutes.
8 Remove from baking tray at once and roll, scroll fashion, while still warm, over the handle of a wooden spoon.

This mixture will make about three dozen.

PECAN SOUP

Pecan Soup:
½ **cup pecan halves**
½ **cup water**
¾ **cup cream**
1 **tablespoon butter**
1 **small onion**
1 **tablespoon flour**
2 **cups chicken stock**
2 **sticks celery**
2 **egg yolks**
extra ¼ **cup cream**

1 Puree pecans and water in blender until smooth.
2 Put in a small saucepan and add cream.
3 Heat gently—do not allow to boil.
4 Allow to stand for at least 15 minutes.
5 Heat butter in a medium saucepan.
6 Add sliced onion and cook gently until tender.
7 Add flour and stir to combine.
8 Remove from heat and stir in chicken stock.
9 Return to heat and stir until sauce boils and thickens.
10 Add the chopped celery and simmer, covered, for 15 minutes.
11 Strain and return to rinsed pan.
12 Add cream and pecan mixture.
13 Beat egg yolks with the extra cream and stir into soup.
14 Reheat, stirring constantly. Do not allow soup to come to the boil.
15 Garnish and sprinkle with chopped parsley.

This recipe serves about six.

AVOCADO PECAN DIP

Avocado Pecan Dip
1 **ripe avocado**
½ **cup sour cream**
½ **cup pecans**
2 **teaspoons finely chopped onion**
¼ **teaspoon salt**
black pepper to taste

1 Cut avocado in half, remove seed and scoop out the flesh, retaining the shell.
2 Blend avocado flesh until smooth.
3 Combine flesh with remaining ingredients and spoon into avocado shell.
4 Chill thoroughly before serving with savoury crackers and rye bread.

YUMMY NUTS

Yummy Nuts:
¼ **cup butter**
½ **teaspoon tabasco**
1 **teaspoon worcestershire**
¾ **tablespoon garlic salt**
¼ **teaspoon nutmeg**
2 **cups pecan halves**

1 Melt butter.
2 Add spices.
3 Add nuts and spoon butter/spice mixture over nuts.
4 Toast in oven at 200°C for 12 minutes until brown, shaking often.
5 Drain on brown paper.

SAVOURY PECAN RICE

1 Fry the chopped bacon until almost cooked.
2 Add oil, chopped shallots, crushed garlic, chopped celery, chopped capsicum, dried oregano (or basil).
3 Saute for three or four minutes or until vegetables are tender, but crisp.
4 Stir in sliced mushrooms, chopped pecans and cooked rice.
5 Toss lightly and cook until just heated through.
6 Season to taste.

Serves four to six

Savoury Pecan Rice:

3 cups cooked brown rice
3 rashers bacon, chopped
1 tablespoon oil
4 finely chopped shallots
1 clove garlic, crushed
1 cup chopped celery
½ cup chopped red capsicum
¼ teaspoon oregano
125 g sliced mushrooms
1 cup pecans
salt and pepper

PECAN CHIFFON PIE

1 Spread pecans on baking tray and bake for 15 minutes in a 120°C oven.
2 Combine brown sugar and one and one third cups plus two tablespoons water.
3 Bring to the boil.
4 Mix cornstarch and one quarter of a cup of water and stir.
5 Pour into boiling brown sugar mixture, beating with a whisk the whole time.
6 When mixture becomes clear and is the consistency of a thick pudding, remove from heat.
7 Beat egg whites until peaks form.
8 Slowly add the hot brown sugar and fold in.
9 Pile lightly into baked pie shells.
10 Whip cream until stiff then add one quarter of a cup sugar and a little vanilla.
11 Spread whipped cream over both pies and garnish with pecans.

Pecan Chiffon Pie:

1 cup pecans
1 cup brown sugar
1⅓ cups water and 2 tablespoons water
4 tablespoons cornstarch
¼ cup water
⅔ cup egg whites
¼ cup sugar
2 baked pie shells (23 cm)
30 ml whipping cream

PECAN PIE

Pecan Pie:

3 large eggs
½ cup sugar
½ teaspoon salt
3 tablespoons melted butter
1 cup dark corn syrup
1 cup chopped pecans
1 unbaked pie shell (23 cm)
whipped cream
pecan halves for decoration

1 Beat eggs lightly.
2 Add sugar, salt, butter, corn syrup and pecans.
3 Stir well to combine.
4 Pour into pie shell.
5 Bake in a moderate (180°C) oven for about one hour or until filling is well-browned and just set.
6 Decorate with whipped cream and pecan halves.

This pie serves eight people — if they are not greedy.

PECAN AND MUSHROOM SALAD

Pecan & Musroom Salad:

125 g mushrooms
2 tablespoons salad oil
1 tablespoon lemon juice
4 shallots
1 cup chopped pecans
1 cup chopped celery
½ cup chopped parsley

1 Brush insides of mushrooms with French dressing.
2 Combine crabmeat or tuna, mayonnaise, finely chopped parsley and shallots or onion and the pecans.
3 Season with salt and pepper to taste.
4 Use approximately one teaspoon of filling in each mushroom.

PECAN CRABMEAT STUFFED MUSHROOMS

Pecan Crabmeat Stuffed Mushrooms:

25 small mushrooms
French dressing
170 g crabmeat or tuna
2 tablespoons mayonnaise
2 tablespoons parsley
2 tablespoons shallots or onion
½ cup chopped pecans
salt and pepper to taste

1 Slice mushrooms into a salad bowl.
2 Combine salad oil and lemon juice.
3 Sprinkle over mushrooms and toss to coat.
4 Add remaining ingredients, stir thoroughly and chill.

Battered Fruit

Question When I try to make fruit fritters the batter won't stick. Where am I going wrong?

Answer Fritters, food coated with batter, must be quickly deep fried in very hot oil (never butter). The cooking of the batter is affected by the boiling of the moisture in the food. For most fritters, the oil should be between 188°C and 195°C. There is a simple temperature test—drop a two cm cube of bread in the oil. It should brown in 40 seconds.

1 Sift together the flour, baking powder and salt.
2 Beat together the egg and milk.
3 Add these to the dry ingredients, adding a little more milk if necessary to make a thin batter mixture.
4 Add the grated orange rind and the melted butter.
5 Douse fruit pieces in the batter.
6 Drop them one by one into the very hot oil in an uncovered and uncrowded pan.
7 Cook till golden brown, turning the fritters as they float to the top.
8 Drain well on kitchen paper and roll in sugar.

Battered Fruit:
1 cup flour
1 teaspoon baking powder
pinch of salt
1 whole egg
¼ cup milk
½ teaspoon grated orange rind
1 tablespoon melted butter
more milk if necessary

ALTERNATIVE FRUIT BATTER

1 Sift the flour and salt into a mixing bowl.
2 Gradually work in the water and oil with a wooden spoon.
3 Beat until smooth.
4 Whisk the egg whites stiffly and fold them evenly and lightly into the batter.
7 Use immediately.

Alternative Batter:
115 g plain flour
pinch of salt
160 ml warm water
1 teaspoon oil or melted butter
2 egg whites

RICH FRITTER BATTER

This is a rich batter and should be made in advance and allowed to mature.

1 Sift flour and salt into a bowl.
2 Make a well in the centre and gradually beat in the egg, beer and brandy with a wooden spoon.
3 Stir until the batter is smooth and fairly thick.

Rich Fritter Batter:
145 g plain flour
pinch of salt
2 egg yolks or 1 whole egg
150 ml light beer
1 tablespoon brandy

Shelling (or Deshelling) Eggs

Question I often have to shell a lot of hard-boiled eggs and I've noticed some are easier to do than others. Are there any tips to make the shelling of hard-boiled eggs easier?

Answer A French tip—remove the egg from the water as soon as it is hard-boiled and gently tap both ends, just breaking the shell. When the egg is cool enough to touch the lips, blow through the cracked ends. Within seconds you should be able to remove the shell easily.

An Aussie tip—lift the egg from the boiling water and gently crush the shell all over. Drop the egg(s) into cold water for a few minutes. The shell should then peel off cleanly.

It is easier to peel the shells from eggs which are a few days old.

Ricotta Cheese

Question I'm rather fond of ricotta cheese and I thought I might save money by making it at home.

Answer Ricotta cheese is very simple to make.

1 Mix one litre of milk with the juice of one small lemon.
2 Heat the milk until it is warm, but not hot.
3 Remove from the heat when the milk begins to curdle and let stand until the whey looks yellowish. If it does not turn yellow, return pan to the heat and add a little more lemon juice.
4 Drain the curd in a cloth-lined sieve until it stops dripping.
5 Season to taste with salt, pepper, chives, capsicums or whatever you fancy.

This ricotta should keep well in the refrigerator for about a week.

Pickled Nasturtium Buds and Seeds

The nasturtium is grown for both decoration and food. Its leaves, petals, buds and seeds are all edible. The leaves and petals are similar to watercress and may be used in the same way. The young buds and seeds are often pickled in vinegar and used to flavour sauces and also as garnishes. Pickled nasturtium buds have a slightly bitter, peppery taste, and may be used in place of capers. Gather nasturtium buds on a dry day and leave them to air for three days.

PICKLED NASTURTIUM BUDS

1 Place vinegar, peppercorns, mustard seeds, coriander seeds and mace in a small saucepan.
2 Bring to boil over high heat for four minutes.
3 Remove from heat and set aside for half an hour.
4 Place nasturtium buds in a large, warmed preserving jar.
5 Strain the spiced vinegar over the buds and leave to cool before sealing the jar.

The buds should be left to mature for two to three months before using.

Pickled Nasturtium Buds:

350 g nasturtium buds

200 ml malt vinegar

5 black peppercorns

5 white peppercorns

1 teaspoon mustard seeds

1 teaspoon coriander seeds

1 blade of mace

PICKLED NASTURTIUM SEEDS

A Pre-1914 Recipe

Gather the seeds on a dry day when they are quite young and soft. Wipe clean with a cloth and put in a dry glass bottle. Cover with the following liquid: to one pint of vinegar add one ounce of salt and six peppercorns. If you have not enough seeds ripe, you can add them from day to day until the bottle is filled. Seal well and resin the corks of the bottles. As they take ten to twelve months to get pickled, they should be made one season for use the next.

Pre-1914 Recipe:

nasturtium seeds

1 pint vinegar

1 oz salt

6 peppercorns

Pickled Nasturtium Buds

PICKLED NASTURTIUM SEEDS

1 Wash seeds and leave to soak overnight in cold water.
2 Mix vinegar and other ingredients, except the seeds.
3 Drain the seeds and put in jars.
4 Cover with the cold spiced vinegar.
5 Cover tightly and keep twelve months before using.

Pickled Nasturtium Seeds:

nasturtium seeds
1 litre vinegar
550 g salt
12 peppercorns
a piece of horseradish root
2 cloves
4 tarragon leaves

Carlings

Question I need a recipe for carlings. My husband is a Tynesider from England and he desperately wants to taste carlings again.

Answer First, let us explain what carlings are and how the dish got its name. Carlings are small brown peas, or parched peas, soaked overnight and served hot with brown sugar and a dash of rum. It is said that the dish is named after a Captain Carling, whose ship, with a load of brown peas aboard, was wrecked on the north coast of England. Captain and crew were rescued by the locals and, in gratitude thereafter, Captain Carling returned each year on the anniversary of his rescue to present the townspeople with a gift of peas. Today, carlings traditionally are eaten on Carling Sunday, originally Palm Sunday, but now the fifth Sunday in Lent. Tynesiders have a saying: 'Tid, Mid, Miserei Carling, Palm, and Paste Egg Day'.

Carlings, or carlins, may be prepared in the following way:

1 Soak the peas overnight.
2 Drain and cook in boiling water, with a pinch of salt, for approximately 20 minutes. **Do not overcook the peas.**
3 Melt the butter in a frypan, add the drained peas and fry for two to three minutes.
4 Serve hot, sprinkled with brown sugar and topped with a dash of rum.

RUSTMARKS

Apply lemon juice to the rust mark and leave for ten to fifteen minutes. Place a damp cloth over the stain and iron. Repeat if necessary. Rinse and wash in a good detergent.

Carlings:

half a pound brown peas
pinch salt
one ounce butter
soft brown sugar
dash of rum

Celery Soup

Not Strictly Celery Soup:

500 g potatoes
1 onion
1 parsnip
1 turnip or swede
½ bunch celery
3 large tablespoons butter
1½ litres water
2 large teaspoons salt
2 large teaspoons sugar
550 ml milk
3 large tablespoons flour
croutons

Question I need a good recipe for cream of celery soup. I've tried several from my collection of cookery books, but they lack something.

Answer There should be at least one among the following selection of celery soup recipes which will please the most fastidious palate.

NOT STRICTLY CELERY SOUP

1 Wash, dry and peel, if necessary, all the vegetables and cut them up roughly.
2 Melt the butter in a large saucepan.
3 Add the vegetables and stir until they steam.
4 Add the water, salt and sugar and simmer for one hour.
5 Cool a little and blend, then return to the saucepan.
6 Blend the flour with a little of the milk.
7 Add the rest of the milk to the saucepan, and then add the flour paste to the soup, stirring until it boils.
8 Cook for three minutes.
9 Serve with croutons and garnish with chopped parsley.

Cream of Celery Soup No 1:

celery, stalk and leaves
1 cup water
1 potato, chopped
2 medium onions, chopped
2 large tablespoons butter
3 tablespoons plain flour
3 cups milk
salt and pepper
chopped parsley
whipped cream

CREAM OF CELERY SOUP NO 1

1 Finely chop enough celery stalk and young leaves to fill three cups.
2 Place in a saucepan together with the water, potato and onions.
3 Simmer, covered, for 45 minutes.
4 Blend the mixture.
5 Melt the butter in a saucepan and add the flour.
6 Stir and cook for one minute (do not brown).
7 Add the vegetable puree and the milk, together with salt and pepper to taste.
8 Stir till the mixture boils, then boil for three minutes.
9 Fold through chopped parsley and serve with a dollop of whipped cream in the centre of each bowl.

CELERY SOUP NO 2

This quantity should be enough to serve all the occupants of a small boarding house or a team of shearers.

1 Boil the rice in the milk until it will pass through a sieve.
2 Grate the celery and chop the leaves finely.
3 Cook in the stock until tender, then add the milk/rice mixture.
4 Season with salt and pepper.
5 Serve sprinkled with chopped chives.

Cream of Celery Soup No 2:

1 cup rice
1.6 litres milk
2 medium bunches celery
1.1 litre white stock made from veal or chicken bones
pepper and salt

CELERY SOUP NO 3

1 Place the celery, onion and bay leaf in a saucepan and barely cover with water.
2 Simmer until the celery is soft.
3 Rub through a sieve or colander.
4 Melt the butter in a saucepan and add the flour.
5 Stir and cook for two minutes. Do not brown.
6 Add the milk and stock and stir till the mixture boils.
7 Add celery puree.
8 Season with salt and pepper and serve with fried croutons.

Do not forget to remove the bay leaf before serving. The bay leaf may be omitted from this recipe—and one quarter teaspoon of grated nutmeg substituted.

Cream of Celery Soup No 3:

1 bunch celery, washed and chopped
1 onion coarsely chopped
1 bay leaf
2 large tablespoons butter
2 large tablespoons flour
550 mls milk
275 mls vegetable stock or water
salt and pepper

CREAM OF CELERY WITH CHEESE

1 Shred celery finely and add to stock.
2 Cook until tender.
3 Add celery salt, mace or nutmeg and pepper.
4 Blend flour with a little of the milk until smooth.
5 Add to the celery stock and stir until the whole lot boils.
6 Simmer for ten minutes.
7 Add the remainder of the milk and bring barely to boiling point.
8 Serve immediately, sprinkled with the grated cheese.

Cream of Celery with Cheese:

550 ml chicken or vegetable stock
1 small bunch celery
1 teaspoon celery salt
550 ml milk
1 tablespoon flour
$\frac{1}{8}$ teaspoon mace or nutmeg
pepper to taste
60 g grated tasty cheddar cheese

Gramma and Tomatoes

GRAMMA PIE

Gramma Pie:

short crust pastry
1½ cups cooked mashed gramma
3 eggs
¾ cup brown sugar
1 cup milk
grated rind and juice of one lemon
½ teaspoon nutmeg
½ teaspoon ground ginger
pinch powdered cloves
2 tablespoons sweet sherry

Note: Gramma, *Cucurbita moschata*, is a type of pumpkin. The fruit is elongated, with orange flesh and skin.

1 Line a 23 cm pie plate with short crust pastry, cover with foil and chill.
2 Combine the gramma with the eggs (less one tablespoon of egg white) and the next seven ingredients.
3 Brush the pastry with the reserved egg white.
4 Carefully spoon the gramma mixture into the pie shell and place in a hot oven.
5 Bake for 15 minutes, then reduce the heat to moderately slow and bake a further 35–40 minutes to set the filling.
6 Serve warm with whipped cream.

BENDIGO TOMATO BALLS

Bendigo Tomato Balls:

230 g peeled tomatoes
460 g potatoes
1 egg yolk
2 heaped tablespoons flour
1 tablespoon butter
1 teaspoon sugar
salt and pepper to taste
additional flour

1 Slice the tomatoes into a saucepan.
2 Add salt, pepper, sugar and butter, cover and simmer until soft and mushy, then puree, either through a sieve, or in a food processor.
3 Peel and boil the potatoes, or use cold mashed potatoes. If freshly cooked, rub them through a sieve or put them through a food mill.
4 Mix potatoes into the tomato puree, stir in the flour, and then the beaten egg yolk.
5 Stand for two or three hours or until cool.
6 Shape into small balls with floured hands, dip in flour, and fry in deep smoking-hot fat. If desired, the balls may be dipped in beaten egg and breadcrumbs after flouring.
7 Serve with grilled bacon or gammon, or with a mixed grill.

from 'The New Standard Cookery Book', edited by Elizabeth Craig Odhams Press Ltd London WC2 (Attempts to trace any copyright holder have been made without success.)

Tamarillos

Question I am overwhelmed with tamarillos. So is everyone else and I can't even give the fruit away. I need some good recipes.

Answer The tamarillo (*Cyphomandra crassifolia*) or tree-tomato makes an excellent jam or chutney. It is a native of Brazil and Peru, much cultivated in New Zealand, the only country to grow it on a commercial scale.

TAMARILLO SAUCE FOR MEAT

1 Skin and slice tamarillos.
2 Peel and chop the apple and onion. Add to tamarillos with lemon juice, rind, sugar and salt.
3 Cook till fruits are tender, then sieve.
4 Season with cayenne and more salt, if necessary.
5 Reheat and serve with pork, ham, lamb, etc.

Note: Do not use a blender or processor with tamarillos. The seeds will break and make the sauce bitter.

Meat Sauce:

4 tamarillos
1 small onion
1 small apple
½ teaspoon grated lemon rind
2 tablespoons lemon juice
2 tablespoons brown sugar
¼ teaspoon salt
pinch cayenne

TAMARILLO SAUCE FOR ICE CREAM

1 Skin tamarillos and slice.
2 Place in pan with water and sugar.
3 Cook until fruit is soft.
4 Sieve, then add orange juice and rind
5 Reheat.
6 Cool, bottle and store in refrigerator.

Ice Cream Sauce:

500 g tamarillos
¼ cup water
½ cup sugar
½ teaspoon grated orange rind
¼ cup orange juice

TAMARILLO JAM

1 Pour boiling water over tamarillos and leave for five minutes.
2 Drain, peel and chop.
3 Put into pan, add water and lemon juice.
4 Bring to boil and simmer for half an hour, mashing fruit occasionally.
5 Bring to boil again and add warmed sugar.
6 Boil rapidly until the jam jells when tested (about one hour).
7 Turn into warm, sterilised jars and seal.

Tamarillo Jam:

1½ kg tamarillos
600 ml water
900 g sugar
juice one lemon

Tamarillo Chutney:

2 kg tamarillos
1 kg onions, chopped
2 teaspoons salt
1 teaspoon cayenne pepper
250 g raisins
3 large apples, diced
1 kg brown sugar
1 teaspoon ground cloves
1 teaspoon peppercorns
1 piece cinnamon stick
1 litre vinegar

TAMARILLO CHUTNEY

1 Pour boiling water over tamarillos and leave for five minutes.
2 Drain, peel and cut tamarillos into thin slices.
3 Place tamarillos with remaining ingredients into a large saucepan.
4 Bring to boil, simmer gently, uncovered, for one and a half to two hours, stirring occasionally.
5 Pour into warm preserving bottles, leaving 12 mm (half an inch) headspace.
6 Put on rubber rings, tops and clips.
7 Place in preserver with warm water.
8 Standard preserving pickle time—70 minutes.

Spiced Tree Tomato Jelly:

7 tamarillos
300 ml cold water
¼ teaspoon cloves
¼ teaspoon cinnamon
3 slices of lemon
4 heaped tablespoons sugar
1 tablespoon lemon juice
3 teaspoons gelatine
90 ml hot water

SPICED TREE TOMATO JELLY

1 Add tamarillos to cold water, with the cloves, cinnamon and lemon slices.
2 Cook gently until fruit is soft.
3 Strain fruit from syrup.
4 Skin fruit and cut into small pieces.
5 Add sugar and lemon juice to strained syrup and boil for five minutes.
6 Return chopped fruit to syrup.
7 Add the gelatine which has been dissolved in hot water.
8 Place in serving dishes and allow to set.

Avocado Desserts

Question We sometimes have avocado with a dressing, at the start of the main meal. Are there other ways of preparing avocado? I think I've heard that it can be used in desserts.

Answer There are many, many different ways of presenting that delightful fruit, the avocado, which is also known as the alligator pear and gets its name from the Spanish *agaucate*, an allusion to the shape of the fruit.

Before we proceed to avocado-based desserts, here is the recipe for Guacamole.

GUACAMOLE

1 Sprinkle a bowl with a little salt and rub it with the cut garlic.
2 Mash the avocado in the bowl.
3 Season with a quarter of a teaspoon of salt, chilli powder and lemon juice.
4 Stir in minced onion. If desired, ripe tomato flesh, diced, may be added; or sliced ripe olives; or crumbled crispy bacon. Mix well.
5 Cover with a thin layer of mayonnaise. This keeps the mixture from darkening.
6 Just before serving, stir well.
7 Serve as a dip or on lettuce, as a salad.

Guacamole:

1 clove garlic, cut
salt
1 large avocado
¼ teaspoon chilli powder
1 teaspoon lemon juice
2 teaspoons minced onion
mayonnaise

AVOCADO EXOTICA

1 Cut avocados in half lengthways.
2 Remove seeds and flesh. Do not damage the skin.
3 Peel mandarins and remove pith. Divide into segments.
4 Dice avocados and bananas and steep in brandy, curacao and sugar. Chill.
5 Blend together with apricot puree and fill avocado shells.
6 Pipe with whipped cream, decorate with cherries and sprinkle with almonds.

Avocado Exotica:

3 avocados
2 bananas
2 mandarins
15 ml brandy
1 teaspoon curacao
sugar
whipped cream
shredded almonds
280 ml apricot puree
maraschino cherries

AVOCADO SOUFFLE

Avocado Souffle:

60 g butter
4 tablespoons flour
1 cup milk
fresh ground nutmeg
fresh ground white pepper
salt
4 eggs separated
2 egg whites
2 very ripe avocados
cream of tartar
250 g cream cheese
juice two lemons
chopped parsley
chopped chives

1 Butter a two litre souffle dish and dust with flour, shaking out excess.
2 Preheat oven to 190°C.
3 Melt butter in saucepan and stir in flour, blending to make a roux.
4 Cook for about five minutes, stirring constantly. Do not let the flour brown.
5 Beat in the milk and continue to stir until sauce is thick and bubbly.
6 Remove from heat.
7 Add salt and pepper to taste and a generous pinch of nutmeg.
8 Allow sauce to cool slightly.
9 Beat the four egg yolks into the cooled bechamel sauce and set aside.
10 Cut avocados lengthways, scoop out flesh and puree.
11 Measure 1½ cups of puree.
12 Combine with bechamel.
13 Place egg whites in a large bowl. Add pinch of salt and pinch of cream of tartar.
14 Whisk egg whites until firm.
15 Whisk about one third of egg whites into egg yolk mixture.
16 Pour this over remaining whites and fold in carefully.
17 Correct seasoning, if necessary, and pour into prepared souffle dish.
18 Place on baking dish and cook in oven for 35 minutes. For a drier souffle, increase cooking time by five to ten minutes.
19 Serve immediately with lemon sauce made by combining 250 g of cream cheese in a blender with three to four tablespoons each of chopped parsley and chives. Add juice of two lemons and season to taste with salt and pepper.

Avocado Fool:

3 large avocados
juice of 1 large lemon
1 tablespoon icing sugar
100 ml cream

AVOCADO FOOL

1 Peel, stone and dice avocado.
2 Blend for 30 seconds with lemon juice and icing sugar.
3 Whip cream and fold into puree.
4 Place in individual serving dishes and chill for two hours.

AVOCADO AND STRAWBERRY MOUSSE

1 Dissolve gelatine in one tablespoon of cold water.
2 Remove flesh from avocado and clean strawberries.
3 Blend avocado and strawberries together, saving a few strawberries for decoration.
4 Add egg yolks, half the sugar and lemon juice and blend again.
5 Whip cream with remaining sugar.
6 Fold two-thirds of the whipped cream into the fruit mixture.
7 Put into individual glasses and chill for at least four hours.
8 Before serving, top with remaining whipped cream and a strawberry.

Serves 4 to 6

Avocado & Strawberry Mousse:

1 ripe avocado
2 punnets of strawberries
4 egg yolks
juice of one lemon
⅓ cup sugar
1 teaspoon gelatine
2 cups of cream, whipped

AVOCADO WHIP

Brazil

1 Mash avocado flesh and add lime juice and sugar.
2 Add ice cream and beat until smooth.
3 Chill.
4 Garnish with brazil nuts.

In Brazil this dish is known as *Abacate Batido.*

Avocado Whip:

1 medium avocado
juice of 1 lime
150 ml vanilla ice cream
2 tablespoons sugar

AVOCADO ICE CREAM

1 Peel and mash avocado with lemon juice.
2 Combine with the rest of the ingredients and partially freeze.
3 Beat mixture until fluffy and smooth.
4 Refreeze.

Avocado Ice Cream:

1 medium avocado
2 tablespoons lemon juice
1 cup orange juice
1 cup cream, whipped
½ cup brown sugar
1 cup milk
1 teaspoon grated lemon rind

Medlar Plums

Question If you are familiar with the medlar plum you will know that it looks like an old witch and is probably one of the ugliest fruits around. We have a medlar plum tree which is loaded with fruit. Can we make jam with the plums?

Answer The medlar plum is similar to the rose hip or crab apple, but is somewhat larger. The botanical name of the medlar plum tree is *Mespilus germanica* and it is described as a small Eurasian rosaceous tree, a native of south east Europe and of what used to be called Persia. The fruit should be picked when green. It is not edible until it has begun to decay and the green colour is gone. This is called bletching. The tree is quite hardy and can be grown in frosty areas.

MEDLAR JAM

Medlar Jam:

2 kg medlar plums
2 litres water
4 lemons
sugar

1 Wash and chop the medlars.
2 Remove a thin peel from the lemons and squeeze out the juice.
3 Put the medlars, the lemon juice and peel in a pan and simmer slowly until the medlars are tender.
4 Sieve the contents of the pan.
5 Allow 340 g of sugar to each 460 g of pulp.
6 Return all to the pan and boil rapidly until the jam reaches the setting point.
7 Bottle in sterilised jars and seal while hot.

Shaddock

PANAMA HATS

Yellowed Panama hats may be whitened by rubbing them with block magnesia.

Question I came across the word shaddock in a book recently. It was a new word for me. I checked it in the dictionary but found little information.

Answer Shaddock is another name for the grapefruit or pomelo, a member of the orange family. The fruit can weigh up to two kilograms. It was named after Captain Shaddock, the man who brought its seeds to Jamaica from the East Indies in 1696. The fruit makes a satisfactory marmalade.

SHADDOCK MARMALADE

1 Wash and cut the shaddocks into very thin slices.
2 Cover with the water and allow to stand for twenty-four hours.
3 Boil the fruit and liquid very slowly until the shaddock slices are tender. This should take about two hours.
4 Add the sugar and the lemon juice.
5 Dissolve the sugar slowly and then boil the lot quickly until the marmalade jells when tested.
6 Allow to cool just a little then pour into warm jars.
7 When the marmalade is quite cold, cover and seal.

Shaddock Marmalade:

2 large shaddocks
6 cups water
1.8 kg heated sugar
juice of two lemons

Pear Mousse

Question We had a very refreshing dessert recently at a restaurant in the Blue Mountains. It was like a frozen mousse, but with the flavour of pears. I'd like to make it at home.

Answer Pear mousse is relatively simple to make.

1 Place half a cup of water in a thick-based pan.
2 Peel, core and slice pears into pan.
3 Add juice and rind of the lemon.
4 Cover pan and simmer gently until pears are tender.
5 Remove lemon rind.
6 Rub pears through sieve with liquid.
7 Soften gelatin in two dessertspoons of cold water for about five minutes.
8 Stir gelatin into still hot pear puree, mixing well.
9 Stir in Grand Marnier or Calvados.
10 When mixture is quite cool, fold in whipped cream.
11 Divide into individual dessert dishes and chill.

Pear Mousse:

6–8 dessert pears
90 g sugar
1 lemon
1 heaped teaspoon powdered gelatin
150 ml whipped cream
1 miniature Grand Marnier or Calvados

Lime Marmalade

Question I've tried making lime marmalade but with little success. The rind is tough when it should be tender. Where am I going wrong?

Answer The lime, *Citrus aurantifolia*, is a small Asian tree with stiff sharp spines. The fruit is small, greenish and round or oval shaped. It is rich in vitamin C. The trick with lime marmalade is to make sure the sugar is not added until after the rind has softened in the cooking process. Limes should not be used when they are still bright green and unripe, otherwise the result will be a very bitter marmalade which is difficult to set (see **pectin**). If the limes are not properly ripe, set them aside until they turn yellowish and are very slightly shrivelled.

BRANDIED LIME MARMALADE

Brandied Lime Marmalade:

1 kg limes (approx 12)
2 litres water
2 kg sugar
½ cup brandy

1 Wash unpeeled limes, then slice as finely as possible.
2 Discard the seeds.
3 Place the limes in a basin with the water and stand overnight.
4 Next day place the lime mixture in a large saucepan, cover and bring to the boil.
5 Reduce heat and simmer, covered, for one hour or until the rind is tender.
6 Measure the liquid. Allow one cup of sugar to each cup of lime mixture.
7 Return lime mixture to saucepan and add sugar.
8 Stir over low heat until sugar is dissolved. The mixture should be no more than 3 cm deep in the pan.
9 Bring to the boil and keep on boil, uncovered, without stirring for 20 to 30 minutes or until the jam will jell when tested on a cold saucer.
10 Stand for five minutes.
11 Stir in brandy.
12 Pour into hot, sterilised jars and seal when cold.

The brandy may be omitted, but we are assured it improves the marmalade immeasurably.

LIME SHRED MARMALADE

1 Peel half of the limes very thinly, taking great care not to remove any of the pith.
2 Chop this rind into fine shreds.
3 Peel remaining limes and place this peel, unshredded, into a muslin bag.
4 Roughly chop all the lime pulp, including the pith, and place in another muslin bag together with the pips. Tie the bags.
5 Place the shredded peel and the water in a preserving pan of a suitable size.
6 Add the two tied muslin bags, cover and stand overnight.
7 Next day, simmer the lot gently for approximately one hour.
8 Remove the muslin bags.
9 Add sugar and lemon juice.
10 Stir over low heat until the sugar is dissolved.
11 Bring to the boil and cook slowly for about 40 minutes or until the marmalade sets when tested.

Lime Shred Marmalade:

450 g limes
1.5 litres water
1 kg sugar
juice one lemon

Mouldy Marmalade

Question I make quite good marmalade most of the time, but sometimes I do strike a problem with mould forming on the surface. How can this be prevented?

Answer Mould may be caused by:

1 Underripe or overripe fruit
2 The setting test having been done incorrectly
3 The jars not having been filled right to the top
4 The lid having been put on jars while the jam or marmalade is warm instead of hot to very hot
5 The jars having been stored in a damp place
6 A space between the jam surface and the lid
7 The jars and tops not having been sterilised properly
8 The lid not having been twisted or clipped on fully.

Marmalade and Jam - the Difference

BLUE PEAS

To cook blue peas soak in cold water overnight, adding a small pinch of bicarbonate of soda. Next morning drain the peas and cover with cold water. Add one teaspoon of cider vinegar and boil till soft. Do not overcook. If left in the cooking water and covered, the peas will continue to cook after they are removed from the heat.

Question What is the difference between marmalade and jam?

Answer According to Item 1570 on page 779 of Mrs Isabella Beeton's *The Book of Household Management*, published in London by Ward, Lock and Co in 1880:

'Marmalades, jams and fruit pastes are of the same nature and are now in very general request. The appellation of marmalade is applied to those confitures which are composed of the firmer fruits, as pineapples, or the rinds of oranges; whereas jams are made of the more juicy berries, such as strawberries, raspberries, currants, mulberries, etc. Fruit pastes are a kind of marmalade, consisting of the pulp of fruits, first evaporated to a proper consistency, and afterward boiled wih sugar. Marmalades and jams are now so cheap that they are within the reach of the poorest. They can also be bought so good that there is little inducement to make them at home if the fruit has to be bought or is dear.' An interesting comment indeed from the extraordinary Mrs Beeton.

A regular *Q&A* correspondent, Bill The Courier, passed on the following: Having been educated in Scotland I was told a nice but probably untrue story. While travelling through Scotland, Mary Queen of Scots stopped at a hostelry for refreshments. She was given scones upon which was some orange jam. The Queen commented to the serving girl how nice it was, whereupon in a thick Scottish brogue, the girl said 'Would ye like some mair Milady?'.

Pectin

Question I know that pectin should be present when making jam and that it is a setting agent. Is it possible to make pectin and add it to jam?

Answer Pectin is the concentrated extract of a group of substances found in the cell walls of certain plants. It is capable of forming thick solutions and therein lies its value as a setting agent in jams and jellies. The chief sources of pectin are citrus waste and the residue from cider presses. Very small amounts of pectin in the presence of fruit acids and sugar suffice to form a jelly.

The following is a test for pectin and a guide to the amount of sugar to be used in jam making. To find out whether fruit holds little or much pectin, after the fruit has boiled to a pulp take a teaspoon of juice and place it in a tumbler. Allow it to cool, then add three teaspoons of methylated spirits, shake slowly and stand for two minutes. If the fruit holds good pectin content, one transparent jelly clot is formed. If this is the case, use equal amounts by weight of sugar to fruit.

If the pectin content is not so good, the single jelly clot may break into two or three clots. In this case, continue boiling the fruit a little longer and reduce the amount of sugar slightly.

To make Pectin: pour boiling water over lemon pips in a cup and allow to soak overnight, then remove the pips. The resulting jelly is heavy with pectin.

Alternatively the seeds may be put in a muslin bag and placed in the jam. The bag should be removed before the jam is bottled.

One teaspoon of citric acid added while making jam is said to be a foolproof method of inducing the jam to jell.

Here is a more elaborate recipe for pectin:

SOAP SCRAPS

Small pieces of soap can be recycled. Cut them into even smaller pieces and use one cup of soap to one cup of water. Add ⅔ cup of rolled oats and soak all together overnight. The following day heat the soap/rolled oats mixture in a saucepan together with one tablespoon of honey. Simmer over a low heat until the scraps are melted, stirring every so often with a wooden spoon. While the mixture is simmering add two tablespoons of glycerine and mix in well. Pour this mixture into a suitable container and allow to set. If you wish, a little perfume may be added before the soap sets.

Pectin:

---

2 kg apples, including skins and cores

2½ litres of water

---

1 Select tart, hard, ripe apples.
2 Remove bruised spots and cut apples into thin slices.
3 Place these in a large enamel pan with the water and bring to the boil quickly.
4 Cover and leave on the boil for 20 minutes.
5 Strain through four thicknesses of cheesecloth.
6 When the juice has stopped running, press the pulp lightly with a spoon. Make sure you do **not** squeeze the pulp.
7 Set aside the juice.
8 Remove the pulp from the cheesecloth and weigh.
9 Add to it an equal quantity of water, boil again for 20 minutes and strain.
10 Mix the two liquids, which should measure about three and a half litres.
11 Place in a wide pan so the mixture is not more than three cm deep.
12 Heat rapidly and reduce to about 1 cm.
13 If not used at once, pour into hot sterilised jars that have been standing in hot water.
14 Seal.

Here are a few tips on jam-making passed on by *Q&A* jam makers.

Extracting pectin from the fruit used for jam making, a most important part of the whole process, is best done when the fruit is just under-ripe. Acid in the fruit helps the extraction. As fruit ripens, the acidity decreases. If over-ripe fruit is used, then extra acid must be supplied. This also applies where the fruit is naturally acid deficient. Fruit in this category includes strawberries, cherries, melon and marrow.

Acid can be supplied in the form of fresh lemon juice, in the order of two tablespoons to one kilogram of fruit, or a small level teaspoon of citric or tartaric acid to the same amount of fruit.

Fruits such as plums, gooseberries and so on are easy to make into jam, because of their high acid and pectin content.

Overboiling leads to candying, darkness in colour, and the destruction of flavour. Underboiling will lead to fermentation, because too little water has been extracted. A deficiency of sugar will also cause fermentation. Sugar is one of nature's best preservatives.

Perfect jam will contain pectin, sugar and acid in exactly the right proportions.

The jam pan must be clean and bright at the start. A little butter rubbed over the surface of the pan before commencing will help prevent the jam sticking. A glass marble may also be placed in the jam. Its movement helps to prevent sticking.

With the exception of strawberries and similar fruits, it is best to boil the fruit before adding the sugar, which should have been warmed in the oven.

Tomato Paste

Question It is possible to make tomato paste at home?

Answer To make approximately one kilogram of tomato paste you will need about five kilograms of tomatoes and two tablespoons of salt. The tomatoes must be ripe and sound with no signs of decay. Wash them well, core out the stem and slice the tomatoes into a large preserving pan. Cover and heat gently until the tomatoes are soft. Rub them through a sieve and return the juice to the pan. Using a moderately low heat reduce the volume by half in the uncovered pan. At this stage you have achieved tomato puree.

To achieve the paste pour the puree into two large pans (baking dishes are fine) and place them in the sun, protected by gauze. Dry out in the sun for two to four days, stirring now and then. Alternatively, place the pans in a cool (100°C) oven for four to six hours.

When the paste is thick enough, stir in the salt and place in sterilised jars. Top with a layer of oil and seal. Store in a cool place. Once the jar is opened, it should be stored in the refrigerator.

STORING BLANKETS

Dissolve a lump of camphor in hot water and add this to the final rinse cycle when washing blankets before storing them for the summer. They will be mothproofed.

Lillipilli Jelly

Question My lillipilli tree is overloaded with fruit at the moment. Is there a recipe for making the fruit into a jam or jelly?

Answer Lillipilli jam is simple to make, with an individual flavour. You will need one cup of heated sugar and one dessertspoon of lemon juice for each cup of lillipilli juice.

Lillipilli Jelly:

lillipillies

water

sugar

lemon juice

1 Wash the lillipillies, cover them with cold water, then boil for one hour.
2 Press the lillipillies down in the pan, then strain the resulting liquid.
3 Add the heated sugar and lemon juice and cook quickly until it jells.
4 Pour into sterilised jars, seal and store in a cool place.

Apricot Health Candy

Apricot Health Candy:

115 g dried apricots

½ cup water

1 teaspoon grated lemon rind

1 teaspoon grated orange rind

⅓ cup blanched chopped almonds

½ cup honey

½ cup skim milk powder

1 teaspoon wheatgerm

½ cup sultanas

½ cup coconut

Question I enjoy eating those health bars which contain dried fruit and I've often wondered whether it is easy to make them. Does someone know?

Answer The following method should provide a satisfactory result.

1 Chop apricots and combine with water.
2 Simmer until tender.
3 Add remaining ingredients.
4 Remove from heat and mix thoroughly.
5 Spread mixture on a lightly greased shallow pan.
6 Refrigerate for several hours.
7 Using a sharp knife, cut into bars.
8 Wrap in wax paper.

Jellied Eels

Question My husband loves jellied eels. I can't stand the thought of them myself, but I would try to prepare them if I had a recipe.

Answer Preparing jellied eel can be a lengthy process. Here are two methods, the first somewhat simpler than the second.

1 Make a court bouillon of the white wine, water, carrots and leeks, by simmering them together for ten minutes.
2 Season to taste with salt and pepper then cool.
3 Skin eels, wash thoroughly, cut into 6 cm pieces and wash again thoroughly, removing all the blood inside near the bone.
4 Drain.
5 Place eel pieces in cool court bouillon and bring rapidly to boil.
6 Reduce to very slow simmer for 30 minutes.
7 Transfer to a suitable earthenware dish and refrigerate.

The stock will set when cold.

Jellied Eels:

2 eels, each 600 grams

1 bottle dry white wine

¾ litre water

300 g carrots (cut into small stars)

300 g leeks (green part) cut in thick strips

1 large bunch dill, cut coarsely

EEL IN ASPIC

A line eel, three to four pounds in weight, should be obtained and kept in running water for two to three days. Kill the eel by cutting its throat. Collect the blood in a glass. The eel should then be skinned.

1 Line a casserole with the sliced onion and bacon rinds and place the whole skinned eel in the casserole, curling it around.
2 Mix the eel's blood with the claret and blend in the soya bean flour.
3 Pour the blood/claret/flour mixture over the eel.
4 Bake in a moderate oven for 12 hours.
5 Cool, then place in the refrigerator.
6 When properly chilled the sauce will have formed a jelly and the eel will be ready to serve.

Eel in Aspic:

1 eel

2 medium onions

rind from six bacon rashers

1 tablespoon soya bean flour

½ pint claret

Eel in Aspic

Smoking Trout is not a Health Hazard

Question My husband arrived home from the Snowy Mountains at the end of a long weekend with a problem—too many trout. He had caught more than we could manage to eat at one sitting. I need some good, varied ways of preparing trout and a method of smoking them.

Answer One can physically 'smoke' fish in a special cooker available from most sporting and camping stores. One can also use pickle and smoke mix, which is usually available in shops where fishing tackle is sold. The special cooker is simple to use. If different types of sawdust are used in the lower part of the smoker the fish acquire different flavours.

SAUTEED TROUT WITH ALMONDS

Season six trout with a little salt and pepper, dip them in milk and then in flour. Saute the trout in about 5 mm of hot oil until golden brown on both sides. Drain the oil from the pan and remove the fish. Add one tablespoon of unsalted butter for each fish and saute half a cup of slivered almonds until they are brown. Pour the butter and almonds over the trout and serve.

Sauteed Trout with Almonds:
6 trout
salt and pepper
milk
flour
oil
unsalted butter
slivered almonds

GOLDEN OAT TROUT

1 Clean and scale the trout.
2 Combine oatmeal, rolled oats, breadcrumbs and add salt and pepper to taste.
3 Roll trout in flour and dip in combined beaten eggs and milk.
4 Coat well with crumb mixture.
5 Heat butter and oil in a large frying pan.
6 Cook trout on both sides until a golden brown and cooked through.
7 Place on a serving platter and top with lemon slices and Parsley Lemon Butter.

Golden Oat Trout:
6 trout
¾ cup fine oatmeal
1 cup rolled oats
1½ cups fresh breadcrumbs
salt and pepper
flour
2 eggs
¼ cup milk
60 g butter
3 tablespoons oil

Parsley Lemon Butter:

125 g butter
1 tablespoon chopped parsley
2 tablespoons lemon juice
1 teaspoon grated lemon rind
salt and pepper

Baked Egg Trout:

6 trout (cleaned)
4 tablespoons raw mushrooms
1 teaspoon parsley
1 teaspoon onion
1 teaspoon chives
1 teaspoon chervil
3 leaves tarragon
2 tablespoons melted butter
4 egg yolks
3 teaspoons brandy
5 tablespoons soft breadcrumbs
5 tablespoons grated Swiss cheese
paprika
6 large onion slices
6 tomato slices
6 mushrooms

Trout with Cream:

6 trout (cleaned)
¼ cup water
juice of two lemons
salt and pepper
3 tablespoons chopped chives
2 teaspoons chopped parsley
⅔ cup heavy cream
fresh breadcrumbs

Parsley Lemon Butter

1 Beat the butter until it is light and creamy.
2 Fold in parsley, lemon juice, lemon rind, salt and pepper.
3 Roll this mixture into a log shape in waxed paper.
4 Refrigerate until firm.
5 Cut into slices.

BAKED EGG TROUT

1 Season the trout to taste with salt and pepper.
2 Line a buttered baking dish with the finely chopped mushrooms, parsley, onion, chives, chervil and the tarragon leaves.
3 Place the trout on the vegetables and herbs.
4 Spoon over them the melted butter.
5 Cover dish with buttered waxed paper and bake in a hot (205°C) oven for ten minutes.
6 Beat the egg yolks and add the brandy.
7 Remove waxed paper and pour egg/brandy mixture over trout.
8 Sprinkle with a mixture of the breadcrumbs and cheese.
9 Top with a little paprika.
10 Return dish to oven and brown the crumbs.
11 Serve the trout in the baking dish.
12 Accompany the fish with a side dish of grilled large onion slices and grilled tomato slices, each topped with a sauteed mushroom.

TROUT WITH CREAM

1 Butter a flameproof platter and arrange the six trout on it.
2 Pour the water and the lemon juice over the trout.
3 Season to taste with salt and pepper.
4 Sprinkle with chopped chives and parsley.
5 Bring the liquid to the boil over a medium heat.
6 Transfer the platter to a moderate (180°C) oven and bake for 12 to 15 minutes, or until the trout are tender.
7 Bring the cream to the boil and pour over trout.
8 Sprinkle with fresh breadcrumbs.
9 Return platter to oven until crumbs are browned.

COLD TROUT WITH CUCUMBER SAUCE

1 Frozen trout should not be thawed. Trim the fins close to the body, leaving the head and tail intact.
2 Place trout in a pan in a single layer.
3 In a separate pan, bring to the boil the water, coarsely chopped parsley, sliced onion, bay leaf, chopped celery and salt.
4 Pour this liquid over the trout.
5 Cook for five minutes—eight minutes if the trout are frozen.
6 Remove from heat and leave in liquid until cool.
7 Carefully lift the trout onto a serving plate and remove the skin.
8 Serve the sauce separately.

Cucumber Sauce

1 Peel the cucumber and halve lengthwise.
2 Scoop out the seeds and finely chop the flesh.
3 Beat the cream until it is thick.
4 Mix cucumber flesh into beaten cream.
5 Season with salt and pepper to taste.
6 Add tarragon vinegar.

Cold Trout with Cucumber Sauce:

4 medium fresh or frozen trout
3 cups water
2 parsley sprigs
½ small onion
1 bay leaf
1 small celery stalk
1 teaspoon salt
Sauce:
2 small or 1 medium cucumber
150 ml cream
salt and pepper
3 tablespoons tarragon vinegar

SMOKED TROUT PATE

1 Skin and bone the trout, remove the flesh and flake it.
2 Beat softened butter on medium speed in mixer until creamy.
3 Add finely chopped onion, trout, cream and a few drops of tabasco.
4 Beat a further two minutes.
5 Season with pepper.
6 Spoon pate into four individual serving dishes and refrigerate.
7 When serving, allow pate to return to room temperature, then serve with Melba toast.

Smoked Trout Pate:

1 smoked trout (300 g)
2 tablespoons chopped onion
250 g butter
2 tablespoons cream
tabasco
ground pepper

Smoked trout may be salty. It is a good idea to use unsalted butter in this recipe. Add a teaspoon of lemon juice, it will enhance the flavour.

Rollmops

Question Is it easy to prepare rollmops?

Answer Perhaps we should explain rollmops. They are herrings treated with herbs and butter. There are variations in the preparation. Jenny Burman found the following in a recipe book which belonged to her mother.

TO PICKLE HERRINGS

Pickled Herrings:

6 salt herrings (2 to have 'milch' or 'pale' roes)
3 medium onions, white preferably
cloves
bay leaves
1½ cups vinegar
2 dessertspoonsful sugar

1 Wash herrings thoroughly, removing roes, and soak with 'milch' roes overnight in cold water.
2 Boil vinegar and let it cool before using.
3 Pound 'milch' roes with sugar until dissolved, then add the vinegar and mix well.
4 Wash herrings again and cut in slices, or fillets, as desired.
5 Slice onions in rings.
6 Place a layer of onions in a jar, a few cloves, and bay leaves.
7 Add a layer of herring closely packed.
8 Continue layers in this order till all used up, with onions the final layer.
9 Pour on the vinegar mixture.
10 If there is insufficient vinegar mixture, add plain vinegar until well covered.
11 Cover jar and place in a cool spot. These will be ready to use in two days.

HERRINGS (SPICED OR SOUSED)

Spiced or Soused Herrings:

4 fresh herring
60 g butter
1 teaspoon made mustard
290 ml vinegar
a sprinkling of salt
½ teasoon ground ginger
6 peppercorns
1 small teaspoon sugar

1 Clean, bone and skin fish.
2 Put fillets of fish in a baking dish.
3 Melt butter and mix with the mustard, salt, sugar and ginger.
4 Add vinegar and pour over the fish.
5 Add peppercorns.
6 Cover and bake in a moderate oven (180°C) until the fish are quite tender.
7 Serve hot or cold.

HERRING ROLLMOPS

1 Soak the herrings in cold water overnight, then drain and clean.
2 Remove skin and separate each fish into two fillets, removing the bones.
3 Mix the remaining ingredients into a smooth paste and spread the paste on each fillet.
4 Roll the pasted fillet and secure with a toothpick or string.
5 Place in a baking dish and cover with oiled paper.
6 Bake in a moderate oven (180°C) for 10 to 15 minutes.
7 Serve hot.

Herring Rollmops:

6 salt herring
2 tablespoons breadcrumbs
2 tablespoons butter
1 tablespoon chopped parsley
1½ tablespoons lemon juice
pepper
hot water

ROLLED PICKLED FILLET OF HERRING

Use pickled herring fillets. Place a small gherkin on each fillet and roll up, fastening same with a wooden toothpick. Use the onions pickled with the herring as a garnish.

Baked Barracouta and Other Fish

BAKED BARRACOUTA

1 Wash and dry the steaks.
2 Mix flour with pepper and salt to taste and dip steaks in flour.
3 Place fish steaks side by side in a buttered baking dish.
4 Sprinkle with parsley and lemon juice and dab thickly with butter.
5 Cover and bake in a moderate (180°C) oven for 30 minutes, or until fish shows signs of coming away from the bones.

Baked Barracouta:

4 medium sized barracouta steaks
salt and pepper to taste
60 g butter
1 teaspoon minced parsley
juice of ½ lemon
flour as required

from 'The New Standard Cookery Book', edited by Elizabeth Craig Odhams Press Ltd London WC2 (Attempts to trace any copyright holder have been made without success.)

BOILED MURRAY COD

Boiled Murray Cod:
1 kg Murray Cod
1½ teaspoons salt
2 tablespoons lemon juice
2 litres water

1 Choose the middle cut for preference.
2 Wash and scrape away any blood from the backbone.
3 Bring water to the boil and add salt and lemon juice.
4 Put in the fish, bring to the simmering point and simmer, allowing 15 minutes for each 500 g.
5 Remove very carefully to a dish lined with a napkin, if it hasn't a drainer.
6 Garnish with slices of lemon.
7 Serve with plain melted butter, or anchovy, egg, parsley, caper or egg and parsley sauce, in a hot sauceboat.

from 'The New Standard Cookery Book', edited by Elizabeth Craig Odhams Press Ltd London WC2 (Attempts to trace any copyright holder have been made without success.)

TRUMPETER DUMPLINGS

Trumpeter Dumplings:
230 g cold boiled Trumpeter
1½ teaspoons minced onion
30 g flour
1 egg
30 g minced bacon
30 g butter
150 ml milk
salt, pepper and paprika

1 Melt the butter in a saucepan and add the bacon and onion. Cook for three or four minutes.
2 Stir in the flour and when frothy, stir in the milk. Bring to the boil, stirring constantly and simmer for five minutes, still stirring.
3 Stir in the beaten egg and flaked fish.
4 Add seasonings to taste, spread on a dish and stand till cool.
5 Shape into small equal sized balls.
6 Place gently in boiling fish stock or water and cook for five minutes.
7 Drain well and serve on a hot dish.
8 Mask each with anchovy or tomato sauce and serve the remainder of the sauce in a hot sauceboat.

Note: These dumplings can be made with any cold fish.

from 'The New Standard Cookery Book', edited by Elizabeth Craig Odhams Press Ltd London WC2 (Attempts to trace any copyright holder have been made without success.)

SHELLFISH STUFFING

1 Chop crayfish meat and prawns.
2 Mix with crumbs, melted butter, beaten egg, salt, pepper, paprika and ground mace to taste. If you like things highly seasoned, add some cayenne pepper.
3 Use for stuffing any white fish. Baste well while baking.
4 Serve with melted butter sauce.

from 'The New Standard Cookery Book', edited by Elizabeth Craig Odhams Press Ltd London WC2 (Attempts to trace any copyright holder have been made without success.)

Shellfish Stuffing:
400 g shelled prawns
30 g breadcrumbs
30 g butter
½ crayfish
1 beaten egg
paprika and ground mace
salt and pepper

Popovers

Question Years ago I saw a film—I don't remember its name—in which a couple of the main characters sat in New York's Central Park eating tuna fish popovers and I've wondered about them. I haven't heard of them since.

Answer Popovers are savoury cakes, often served in the US at meals in place of rolls or bread. No skill is required in mixing popovers—success lies in correct baking. Popovers can be baked in heavy aluminium pans and oven-glass or earthenware cups, such as custard cups. The cups should be deeper than they are wide. Metal cups need not be preheated. Glass or earthenware cups should be heated while the batter is being mixed. The batter is thin—about the consistency of heavy cream. The large amount of liquid forms a lot of steam in a hot oven causing the flour and egg mixture to expand and form a hollow shell. The shell is baked until rigid to prevent collapse on cooling.

1 Heat the popover cups in a hot (210°C) oven then remove and grease before filling.
2 Beat all ingredients until mixture is very smooth and fill cups a little less than half full.
3 Bake in preheated oven for about 35 minutes.
4 Resist **all** temptations to **peek**.

The popovers in the movie were probably filled with a tuna mixture.

Popovers:
1 cup sifted plain flour
1 cup milk
½ teaspoon salt
1 tablespoon salad oil
2 eggs

Indian Lime Pickle

Indian Lime Pickle:

20 whole limes
6 tablespoons coarse rock salt
175 g fresh root ginger
300 ml lime juice
20 green chillies
4 bay leaves, crumbled

Question I'm very fond of Indian curries and like to make my own at home. I would like to serve a good lime pickle with the curry but I don't have the real, genuine, original recipe.

Answer This is a complicated and time consuming method of making Indian lime pickle, but the results, if you are a curry fancier, are worth the trouble.

1 Wash the limes in cold water and dry them on paper towels.
2 Using a silver or stainless steel knife make four cuts through the limes, quartering them to within 5 mm of the bottom of the fruit. Remove pips.
3 Slit the green chillies lengthwise and scrape out the seeds, leaving them whole with their stalks.
4 Arrange a layer of limes on the bottom of a large pickling jar.
5 Sprinkle with salt and crumbled bay leaves.
6 Add two or three chillies.
7 Peel and cut the fresh ginger root into matchsticks and add about two tablespoons of the ginger to the jar.
8 Repeat the layering process until all the ingredients, except half the salt, are used up.
9 Pour in the lime juice and shake the jar to settle the contents.
10 Cover the mouth of the jar with a clean cloth and tie it in place with string.
11 Place the jar in a sunny place for six days, adding half a teaspoon of the salt each day.
12 Shake the jar at least twice a day. Each night place the jar in a dry place in the kitchen and be sure to turn the jar each day so that all sides are exposed to the sun's rays.
13 After six days set aside the pickle jar on a shelf for a further ten days.
14 Cover the jar with a lid and shake every day. After ten days the pickle will be ready to eat.

Be warned ... this is a very hot pickle, delightful with Indian curry.

Piccalilli

Question Is piccalilli easy to make?

Answer Yes. Piccalilli is a traditional English mustard pickle, made from a variety of vegetables which are first soaked in brine, then pickled in vinegar. The finished pickle is yellow in colour. This is due to the presence of turmeric and mustard. Piccalilli may be served immediately it has cooled. However, it does improve with keeping and may be stored for up to three months. The pickle is usually served with cold meats.

Use porcelain, enamelled or stainless steel saucepans for pickling. On no account use brass, copper or tin pans. Use wooden spoons for mixing and allow no metallic substance to come into contact with pickle or vinegar. If you put a piece of horseradish into a jar of pickles the vinegar will not lose its strength as quickly and the pickles will keep sound much longer, especially tomato pickles. Always make certain that the vinegar completely covers the pickles. Corks or hot wax are better sealers for pickles than metal lids.

PICCALILLI ONE

Brine: Make enough brine to cover the vegetables. Use 50 g of salt to each 600 ml of water—600 ml is about sufficient for 500 g of vegetables.

1 Wash all the vegetables and the apples, and cut into neat pieces.
2 Cover with cold brine and leave overnight.
3 Drain and pack into jars which have been sterilised and which are still hot.
4 Boil the chilli peppers, garlic, ginger and peppercorns in the vinegar for about five minutes.
5 Add the cornflour, turmeric, and dry mustard, which have been blended previously with a little cold vinegar.
6 Stir and boil slowly for ten minutes.
7 Pour onto the vegetables and fruit and cover in the usual way.

HYDRANGEAS

The blooms of the hydrangea will keep longer if a little eucalyptus is added to the water.

Piccalilli One:

1 large cauliflower
2 green cucumbers
900 g small white onions
900 g apples
25 g chilli peppers
50 g garlic, skinned
25 g bruised root ginger
25 g black peppercorns
1.1 litres white vinegar
50 g cornflour
25 g turmeric
25 g dry mustard

When filling the pickle jars, allow at least 15 mm of liquid above the level of the pickles as a little evaporation is inevitable. However, do not let the vinegar come in contact with metal caps. Allow pickles to mature for at least three months. Preserve the colour by storing in a dark place.

PICCALILLI TWO

Lincolnshire Style

Piccalilli Two:

1 medium marrow
2 small cucumbers
2 small cauliflowers
450 g pickling onions
4 chillies
4 peppercorns
4 cloves
1 tablespoon ginger
1 tablespoon dry mustard
15 g turmeric powder
1 litre vinegar

1 Cut the vegetables into cubes about 20 mm square.
2 Spread them on a platter, sprinkle with salt and leave overnight.
3 Drain off all the water in the morning and wipe dry.
4 Place the vegetables, together with the dry ingredients in a saucepan.
5 Add one litre of vinegar.
6 Boil until the vegetables are tender, about one hour. Stir occasionally to prevent burning.
7 Put into sterilised jars while still warm and seal in the usual way.

PICCALILLI THREE

Piccalilli Three:

1½ kg green tomatoes
¼ cabbage
2 large green cucumbers
4 onions
salt
1 litre vinegar
500 g brown sugar
2 teaspoons turmeric
15 g mustard seeds
10 g celery seeds
½ teaspoon black pepper
10 g dry mustard
¼ cup olive oil

1 Cut the vegetables into 20 mm cubes.
2 Layer them in a basin, alternating with layers of salt.
3 Let stand overnight.
4 Drain, discarding the liquid.
5 Heat the vinegar, sugar and turmeric, together with the seeds and pepper, which have been tied in a muslin bag.
6 Pour over the vegetables and allow to stand for 48 hours.
7 Drain off the liquor and remove the bag of spices.
8 Mix the mustard with the liquor and olive oil and pour over the vegetables.
9 Pack in sterilised jars and cover, using corks which have been dipped in melted wax.

PICCALILLI FOUR

50-Year-Old Recipe

Prepare the vegetables as follows:

Slice a closely grown white-hearted cabbage. Slice a good, sound beetroot. Divide a cauliflower into neat pieces. Trim and wipe a few French beans, gherkins and radishes. Lay these on a sieve, sprinkle well with salt and expose them to the sun or fire for three days—that all the water may be extracted. Shake off the salt and put the vegetables into a stoneware pan. Mix them well and scatter some mustard seed in also. Set some vinegar to boil with one ounce of sliced garlic and ½ ounce of turmeric to each quart. Put the vegetables in a large jar and when the vinegar boils, pour it over them, boiling hot. Tie a paper over the jar and let all stand for two weeks in a warm place, preferably near a fire. Now put the pickle into the jars, but the quantity of the vinegar must be such that it does not fill them. Boil some fresh vinegar with ½ oz white pepper, ½ oz mace and a small pinch of nutmeg and cloves to each quart. When boiling, skim well, and fill the jars. Cover with corks or hot wax.

MUSHROOMS

To distinguish mushrooms from poisonous fungi sprinkle a little salt on the spongy part or gills. If they turn yellow, they are poisonous, if black they are wholesome.
(circa 1890)

Irish Potato Pancakes

Boxty (*Irish Potato Pancakes*) is a traditional dish from Donegal, eaten on the eve of All Saints Day.

1 Peel the raw potatoes and grate them coarsely, then wring in a cloth.
2 Mix with the mashed potatoes and beat in the eggs with a wooden spoon.
3 Add the flour and seasonings, onion and milk and stir to combine.
4 Drop large spoonsful into hot butter and cook for three to four minutes on each side, until crisp and golden.
5 Serve immediately.

Irish Potato Pancakes:

230 g potatoes, raw
230 g potatoes, boiled and mashed
2 eggs
2 tablespoons plain flour
1 teaspoon salt
½ teaspoon fresh ground black pepper
1 small onion, grated finely
¼ cup milk
60 g butter

VARIATION

Variation:
4 cups of peeled and grated potatoes (about 1 kg)
1⅓ cups plain flour
2 teaspoons salt
6 tablespoons milk
2 tablespoons butter
¼ cup brown sugar
4 tablespoons melted butter

1 Squeeze the grated potatoes as dry as possible in a cloth.
2 Combine the potatoes, flour and salt and stir in the milk gradually, using just enough to make the mixture hold together.
3 Let this mixture stand for one hour.
4 Heat a 25 cm heavy frying pan until very hot, then drop in the butter and let it melt.
5 Spread the potato mixture into the pan evenly with a spatula and cook over medium heat until the underside is set and golden.
6 Slide the pancake onto a plate then invert it back into the frypan and cook until the other side is also brown.
7 Serve the pancake straight from the pan with brown sugar and melted butter.

Pickled Cucumbers

Pickled Cucumbers:
4 large cucumbers
¼ cup salt
¾ cup sugar
2 teaspoons mustard seeds
1½ cups white vinegar
½ small red pepper
1 cup water

Question I'm very fond of pickled cucumbers and I'd like to make my own. What's the best recipe?

Answer Bread and Butter Cucumbers are among the most popular pickles. They are easy to make.

1 Wash the cucumbers and slice as thinly as possible.
2 Arrange slices in layers in a large shallow dish, sprinkling a little salt on each layer.
3 Cover dish with kitchen wrap and allow to stand overnight.
4 Drain and rinse cucumber slices well under cold running water, then drain again.
5 In a large saucepan combine the vinegar, water, sugar, mustard seeds, and one teaspoon of salt.
6 Stir until sugar dissolves.
7 Bring to the boil, reduce heat and simmer uncovered for five minutes.

8 Add cucumbers, return to the boil and then remove from the heat.

9 Using tongs, quickly pack the cucumber slices tightly into hot, sterilised jars.

10 Add a few thin strips of red pepper to each jar.

11 Using the vinegar mixture in which the cucumbers were heated, fill the jars to within 1 cm of the top.

12 Seal when cold.

13 Store in a cool, dark place.

If you are **really** fond of pickles, the following method will provide a larger stock.

1 Slice the cucumbers into a large plastic or stainless steel bowl.

2 Add thinly sliced onions and salt.

3 Cover with cold water and stir to mix.

4 Leave to stand for 12 to 24 hours.

5 Drain well.

6 In a large saucepan mix the sugar, mustard seeds, celery seeds and turmeric. Use more turmeric if a bright yellow colour is desired.

7 Add vinegar.

8 Bring liquid to the boil, stirring to dissolve the sugar.

9 Add drained cucumbers.

10 Return to the boil then remove from heat.

11 Sterilise jars in very hot water or in oven.

12 Prepare lids by pouring boiling water over them and leaving them to stand in this until ready for use.

13 Pour cucumber mixture into jars, leaving 1 cm head space.

14 Screw lid firmly on each jar as it is filled.

15 Stand jars on newspapers or folded towels until cold.

16 Wipe clean and store in a cool, dark place.

Wait one to two weeks before using pickles. Keep opened jars in refrigerator.

Pickled Cucumbers Two:

10–12 cups thinly sliced cucumbers
6 onions
½ cup salt
4 cups sugar
1 tablespoon mustard seeds
2 teaspoons celery seeds
1 to 2 teaspoons turmeric
4 cups white vinegar

Pickled Onions

Question I love pickled onions. However, when I prepare my own the centres turn brown. What am I doing wrong?

Answer The method below should eliminate the browning centre problem.

Pickled Onions:

2 kg small onions
750 g salt
5 cups white vinegar
1½ teaspoons whole allspice
4 teaspoons salt
6 whole peppercorns
2.5 cm cinnamon stick
2 teaspoons ground ginger
1½ teaspoons whole cloves

1 Place unpeeled onions and the salt in a large bowl; add enough water to cover and let stand for two days, stirring occasionally.
2 Drain off liquid and use a small, sharp knife to peel the onions, taking care to leave the ends intact so that the onions do not fall apart during the pickling process.
3 Put peeled onions in a bowl and cover with boiling water—let stand for three minutes then drain.
4 Repeat this boiling water/draining process twice.
5 Pack onions into hot jars which have been sterilised.
6 Combine all remaining ingredients in a saucepan and bring to the boil slowly, then reduce heat and simmer for ten minutes.
7 Cool slightly, then strain and pour over onions.
8 Seal the jars.

The pickles can be eaten the next day, but they improve with a standing time of two to three weeks.

Unusual Recipes

TO ROAST AN UDDER
From 'The Good Housewife', 1756

When an udder is to be roasted, the best way is to par-boil it first, then stick ten cloves about it and put it on the spit. Baste it well with butter until it is enough. For sauce put some gravy in one bowl and some sweet sauce in another. It eats very well.

SHEEP'S HEAD SAUTE

1 Boil the head, then cut the meat into small dice-shaped pieces.
2 Dust with a little seasoned flour and the parsley which has been chopped very fine.
3 Put some butter in a pan, toss in the meat and allow to brown. Keep shaking the pan so the meat does not burn.
4 Pour the sherry over and allow to cook for five minutes.
5 Serve very hot, with mashed potatoes.

Sheep's Head Sauté:

1 sheep's head
a little parsley
seasoned flour
butter
½ glass of sherry wine

From the 'Como Cookery Book', reprinted by courtesy of The National Trust of Australia

KANGAROO STEAMER

Prize recipe at the 1862 Exhibition

Take the most tender part of the kangaroo—being careful to remove all the sinews. Chop it very fine with the same quantity of fat, well-smoked bacon. Season with finely powdered marjoram, pepper and a little salt. Let it stew for two hours, then pack or press down in open-mouthed glass bottles. The bung must be sealed down and the outside of the bottles washed down with beaten white of egg. Preserved this way it will keep good for 12 months or more. When needed for use, the vessel containing the preserve should be put into a saucepan of cold water and allowed to boil for 15 minutes (if a large bottle). When dished, pour a little brown gravy, richly flavoured with mace, pepper and salt and garnish with forcemeat balls.

Mrs Sarah Crouch, the Lady of the Respected Under-Sheriff of Tasmania, obtained the prize and allowed the recipe to become public. The dish was partaken of by guests of the Acclimatisation Society at the London dinner that year. Lord Stanley was in the chair. Sir John Maxwell, a first-rate judge, pronounced it excellent as a stew, and said he would like to see it introduced to the navy.

Prince Napoleon, one of the first gastronomers of the day, was desirous to acclimatise the kangaroo to France for the sake of the cuisine the animal affords.

from the 'Como Cookery Book', reprinted by courtesy of The National Trust of Australia

COCKROACHES

Keep a hedgehog in the kitchen and, generally speaking, this animal soon removes the intruders. (circa 1850)

SUNSTROKE

Immediately bruise horseradish and apply it to the stomach and give him gin to drink. Never fails. (circa 1890)

STEAMED KANGAROO OR WALLABY

Steamed Kangaroo or Wallaby:

kangaroo or wallaby meat
salt pork or bacon
2 or 3 onions
½ wineglass of ketchup
1 claret glass of port wine
pepper, salt

1. Cut the kangaroo or wallaby meat into pieces about the size of a small veal cutlet and slice the pork or bacon.
2. Put a layer of pork at the bottom of a boiler or earthenware jar, then a layer of kangaroo, then onions. Season with plenty of pepper.
3. Continue these layers until the meat and onions are all used.
4. Cover with a cloth and then put on the lid, making sure it fits well, so that no steam escapes.
5. Put the pot in a saucepan half full of boiling water and cook for three hours.
6. Half an hour before serving add the ketchup and 20 minutes afterwards the port wine.
7. Serve with a dish of boiled rice.

STEWED BANDICOOT

Stewed Bandicoot:

1 bandicoot
570 ml tomato puree
beef stock
1 tablespoon chopped onion
1 teaspoon lemon juice
60 g bacon fat or dripping
30 g flour
60 g butter
1 teaspoon sugar
salt and pepper to taste

1. Wash and dry the bandicoot and joint.
2. Melt bacon fat or dripping in a saucepan.
3. Dip bandicoot joints in seasoned flour and fry till browned all over.
4. Drain off the fat and add the onion and enough beef stock to just barely cover the bandicoot.
5. Cover with a closely fitting lid and simmer for one and a half hours.
6. Meanwhile, melt butter in another saucepan and stir in the flour. Cook until nutty brown.
7. Stir in tomato puree.
8. Remove cooked bandicoot to a hot platter.
9. Strain stock and measure off 500 ml then stir in the tomato sauce. Stir till boiling.
10. Season to taste with salt, pepper, sugar, and lemon juice.
11. Add the bandicoot, reheat and serve.

from 'The New Standard Cookery Book', edited by Elizabeth Craig Odhams Press Ltd London WC2 (Attempts to trace any copyright holder have been made without success.)

Protected Recipes

The following recipes, from the days before conservation, are included for their historical interest. Most fauna mentioned are protected.

CASSEROLE OF MALLEE HEN

1 Pluck and clean the Mallee Hen.
2 Remove the rind from the bacon, chop it lightly and fry, then turn into a casserole with the fat.
3 Rub bird with seasoned flour and place on the bed of bacon.
4 Arrange pricked sausages and sliced mushrooms around the bird. If preferred, stuff bird with sausage meat or liver forcemeat and omit sausages.
5 Cover casserole and cook in a rather slow oven for one and a half hours. Add stock and wine.
6 Cook, covered, for another ten minutes.
7 Serve with whole new or mashed potatoes, and an orange or orange mint salad.

Casserole of Mallee Hen:

1 mallee hen
230 g small pork sausages
salt and pepper to taste
150 ml white wine
6 rashers of bacon
230 g peeled mushrooms
150 ml stock
flour and paprika

from 'The New Standard Cookery Book', edited by Elizabeth Craig Odhams Press Ltd London WC2 (Attempts to trace any copyright holder have been made without success.)

STURT'S HOT POT

Slice the top off a pumpkin and hollow out the inside. Fill the shell with joints of possum, kangaroo or other meats and replace the lid. Bury the pumpkin in a bed of hot coals and cook till done.

ROAST BLACK SWAN

Choose a young bird and stuff and roast as you would a goose. Pork sausagemeat is the best stuffing. Truss like a goose, brush with lemon juice, cover the breast with rashers of bacon and roast for two hours in a moderate oven. When nearly done, remove rashers, dredge with flour and baste with melted butter or bacon fat till crisp and brown. Serve with apple sauce and with stewed red cabbage. A good sized bird should be enough for eight persons.

from 'The New Standard Cookery Book', edited by Elizabeth Craig Oldhams Press Ltd London WC2 (Attempts to trace any copyright holder have been made without success.)

Sturt's Hot Pot

Very Australian Recipes

DAMPER

1 Sift together the flour and salt.
2 Add the butter and rub in well.
3 Add the milk all at once to a well made in the centre of the flour mixture.
4 Mix well and knead about ten times. If dough is too stiff add a little more milk.

Damper:
3 tablespoons butter
2 cups SR flour
⅔ cup milk
1 teaspoon salt

Traditionally, damper is rolled into balls and cooked in the hot ashes of the campfire. When cooked, the ashy exterior is blown off and the hot bread eaten.

Another method of cooking damper is to peel green sticks as thick as the thumb and grease about 15 cm at the end. The dough is patted out to about 1 cm thick and strips are wrapped around the end of the stick. These are held over the hot coals until they are light brown on the outside and cooked through. When taken off the stick, the hollow centre is filled with butter and jam.

FAIR DINKUM DAMPER

1 Sift flour and salt into a bowl.
2 Add the warm milk and mix with a knife until the dough leaves the sides of the bowl clean.
3 Place dough on greased and floured baking tray.
4 Bake on the bottom shelf of a hot (205°C) oven for half an hour till brown.

Fair Dinkum Damper:
3 cups SR flour
1 teaspoon salt
1¼ cups warm milk

EMU EGG OMELETTE

1 Beat the emu egg, after you have chiselled through the shell and developed Dizzy Gillespie-type cheeks from blowing the contents out of the shell.
2 Add the milk and salt to taste.
3 Fold in the flour with an egg whisk or fork.
4 Pour into a pan in which the butter has already been well heated.
5 When set, spread half with cooked onion, tomato and bacon, then fold over to cover.

Emu Egg Omelette:
1 fresh emu egg (scarce)
1 tablespoon SR flour
tomato
onion
½ cup milk
1 level teaspoon salt
bacon

BACK O'BOURKE

1 Chop two sheep's kidneys very fine.
2 Fry in a saucepan with a little butter until very brown.
3 Shake in a little flour, Worcestershire Sauce, pepper and salt.
4 Bring to the boil and add a little cream.
5 Serve on thick buttered toast.

RABBIT PIE

Rabbit Pie:
2 rabbits, jointed
1 tablespoon vinegar
1 onion, sliced
salt and pepper
250 g streaky bacon
6 chicken livers
½ teaspoon ground mace or nutmeg
1 teaspoon salt
4 tablespoons chopped parsley
1 teaspoon chopped sage
½ cup red wine
125 g butter
185 g puff pastry
beaten egg to glaze

1 Soak rabbits for at least two hours in water to cover, with the vinegar.
2 Drain and place in a saucepan with fresh water to cover.
3 Add the sliced onion, salt and pepper.
4 Bring slowly to the boil, reduce the heat, cover and simmer gently for about 15 minutes.
5 Drain, remove the flesh from the bones and cut into cubes.
6 Chop the bacon, reserving three of the rashers for the top of the pie.
7 Chop the chicken livers finely and beat with half the chopped bacon, mace, salt, pepper, parsley and sage.
8 Line the base of a deep pie dish with the chicken liver mixture.
9 Place the cubed rabbit in the dish and pour the wine over.
10 Cream the butter and mix with the remaining chopped bacon. Spread over the rabbit.
11 Remove the rind from the reserved rashers of bacon, cut into quarters and place on top.
12 Roll out the pastry on a lightly floured surface. Cut a narrow strip to press around the pie plate and brush with a little water.
13 Top the pie with the rolled out pastry, pressing the edges against the pastry strip. Trim the edges and crimp.
14 Make a small cut on the top of the pie to allow steam to escape and brush the pastry with beaten egg.
15 Bake in a moderate (180°C) oven for one hour, or until the pastry is golden and crisp.

BARWON BUNNY

1 Joint and soak rabbits in salted water for half an hour.
2 In a shallow ovenware dish mix one cup of the breadcrumbs, the milk, chopped onion, salt and ground cloves.
3 Place the rabbit on this mixture.
4 Top each piece of rabbit with a rasher of bacon and a slice of tomato.
5 Sprinkle a little brown sugar and salt on the tomato.
6 Cover with the remaining breadcrumbs and last of all put the bacon rinds on top.
7 Bake in a moderate (180°C) oven for about one hour.

from the 'Como Cookery Book', reprinted by courtesy of The National Trust of Australia

Barwon Bunny:
2 young rabbits
1 cup milk
1½ cups breadcrumbs
¼ eggspoon ground cloves
6 rashers bacon
1 medium onion
salt
1 large tomato
brown sugar
bacon rinds

YABBIES

To remove the muddy flavour from yabbies, place them in a bucket of water with 120 grams of Epsom Salts for four hours.

To prepare yabbies for eating: Place all ingredients in a large pot and bring to the boil slowly. Remove the yabbies as soon as the colour changes. Cool and serve with mayonnaise, thinned with lemon juice or French dressing and with two minced hard boiled egg yolks added.

Yabbies:
24 yabbies
2½ l water
1 tablespoon salt
1 tablespoon sugar
1 tablespoon vinegar
mayonnaise or French dressing
2 hard boiled egg yolks

HUNTER VALLEY CASSEROLE

1 Place half the potato slices in a greased casserole dish.
2 Cut the meat into cubes, roll in flour and saute in a little butter.
3 Add the meat to the casserole and cover with onions and mushrooms.
4 Add salt, pepper and wine.
5 Place the remaining potatoes on top, covering the meat completely.
6 Brush with melted butter.
7 Cook in a moderate (180°C) oven for two hours.

Hunter Valley Casserole:
6 potatoes, peeled and sliced
800 g lamb shoulder or breast
2 lamb kidneys, diced
115 g sliced mushrooms
2 tablespoons butter
1 large sliced onion, sauteed in butter
salt and pepper
1 large cup red wine (Hunter Valley, of course)

KANGAROO TAIL SOUP

Kangaroo Tail Soup:

1 kangaroo tail, skinned and jointed
½ cup pearl barley
1 large onion
1 swede turnip
1 parsnip
4 carrots
salt

1 Peel and dice the vegetables.
2 Place them, together with the tail and the pearl barley, in a large boiler and cover with water.
3 Simmer all day.
4 Remove from the heat at night to set the fat.
5 Skim the fat the next morning.
6 Return to the stove and add the seasonings.
7 Serve boiling hot with more vegetables, if desired.

This stew is very rich.

STUFFED NULLARBOR LAMB

Stuffed Nullarbor Lamb:

1 boned leg of lamb
230 g prunes, stoned and chopped
230 g bacon, diced
salt and pepper
½ level teaspoon dry mustard
1½ cups soft breadcrumbs
pinch dried herbs
2 eggs
2 tablespoons oil
2 tablespoons honey

1 Combine prunes with bacon, salt, pepper, mustard, breadcrumbs, herbs and eggs.
2 Stuff leg and truss or sew up.
3 Place in a baking dish; warm the honey and oil slightly and pour over the meat.
4 Cook in a moderate (180°C) oven for 30 minutes per 500 grams.
5 Slice and serve with baked potatoes, minted peas and carrots.

PORT ADELAIDE PIE

Port Adelaide Pie:

12 paroquets or parakeets
6 thin slices pork or beef
salt and pepper
pinch of crushed herbs
4 rashers bacon
½ teaspoon minced parsley
3 hard boiled eggs
water or chicken stock
120 g peeled mushrooms
flour
quantity of puff pastry

1 Prepare and truss birds like quails.
2 Line a pie dish with the pork or beef and place six of the birds on top.
3 Pack slices of egg and pieces of chopped mushroom between, then sprinkle with parsley, herbs and salt and pepper to taste. A suspicion of lemon zest may be added, if desired.
4 Dredge lightly with flour and cover with strips of bacon.
5 Repeat layers and seasonings.
6 Fill dish two thirds full with water or chicken stock.
7 Cover with puff pastry and bake in a hot oven.

from 'The New Standard Cookery Book', edited by Elizabeth Craig Odhams Press Ltd London WC2 (Attempts to trace any copyright holder have been made without success.

No Fat or Low Fat Ice Cream

Question I need recipes for ice creams which do not contain any dairy products. These are for a child with an allergy problem.

Answer The following recipes contain no dairy products, artificial colourings or flavouring agents.

VANILLA ICE CREAM

Soak one level teaspoon of agar-agar * flakes in one cup of water for one minute. Boil for one minute and cool for one minute.

1 Place the agar-agar solution, cashews, water and soy milk powder in a food processor or blender and liquefy till smooth.
2 Add the honey, vanilla to taste, salt (if using) and blend.
3 Add the oil slowly while blending and blend for a further one minute.
4 Freeze in a bowl or tray.
5 Serve before ice cream becomes too hard.

Agar-agar may be bought at Health Food shops.

Vanilla Ice Cream:

1 teaspoon agar-agar flakes
1 cup cashew nuts
2 cups of water
3 tablespoons soy milk powder
½ cup light honey
⅓ cup soy or coconut oil
¼ teaspoon salt (optional)
vanilla extract

STRAWBERRY ICE CREAM

1 Combine strawberries and honey.
2 Cover and chill for one hour.
3 Place the water and soy milk powder in a blender and liquefy until smooth.
4 Add egg yolks and blend again.
5 Add oil slowly at high speed, then blend at high speed until mixture is thick and smooth.
6 Add strawberry–honey mixture and mix well.
7 Pour mixture into chilled ice cream trays.
8 Freeze until mixture is solid around the edges and mushy in the middle.
9 Blend again, then return to trays.
10 Repeat freezing and blending once more.

Strawberry Ice Cream:

2 cups strawberries, washed and sliced
1 cup honey
1 cup ice-cold water
1 cup soy-milk powder
2 egg yolks
½ cup chilled salad oil

PENGUIN ICE CREAM

Penguin Ice Cream:

6 large very ripe bananas

3 tablespoons maple syrup or 2 tablespoons honey

⅓ cup water

4 tablespoons soy milk powder

2 tablespoons fine carob powder

1 Place all ingredients in blender and blend thoroughly.
2 When liquefied, pour into bowl, cover and freeze.

This mixture should not require a second beating and freezing. The carob powder may be replaced with a handful of pitted dates or soaked seedless raisins.

MANGO OR PEACH SHERBERT

Mango or Peach Sherbert:

1 cup pineapple juice

1 teaspoon lemon juice

1½ cups coconut shreds or cashew nuts

1 teaspoon slippery elm*

⅔ cup honey

¼ cup soy or coconut oil

pinch salt

½ cup of mango or 2 cups fresh peaches

Soak one tablespoon of agar-agar* flakes in one cup of water for one minute, then boil for one minute and cool for one minute.

1 Blend pineapple juice and coconut or cashew nuts till smooth.
2 Add agar-agar solution, lemon juice, slippery elm, honey, oil, salt and fruit.
3 Blend again until smooth.
4 Freeze and serve before it becomes too hard.

Items such as agar agar and slippery elm may be bought from Health Food shops.

RAW NUT ICE CREAM

Raw Nut Ice Cream:

2 cups soy milk

½ cup sunflower seeds

½ cup honey

1 teaspoon vanilla

1 cup almonds

½ cup sesame seeds

¼ cup oil

1 Mix all ingredients together and blend in batches until mixture is smooth.
2 Freeze in trays.

This should yield six to eight servings.

Honey Sugar

Question Is honey a healthy food or does it contain just as much sugar as sugar?

Answer Honey, like white sugar, is high in carbohydrate and in kilojoules. It does contain traces of a number of minerals, as well as Vitamins B2, B6, C, H and K. Honey is sometimes used as a substitute for sugar—it contains forty per cent levulose, thirty-four per cent dextrose and two per cent sucrose. It contains eighteen per cent water and also has the capacity to retain water. Cakes, biscuits and icings made with honey remain moister for a longer time than similar products made with most sweeteners. Honey is an easily digestible food which may act as a mild laxative. It has no extra nutritive value and contains only minute traces of calcium, iron and thiamine. According to the Honey Research Institute in Bremen, West Germany, it acts as a disinfectant for the mouth and throat and aids in the relief of colds. Many false claims have been made about honey and its 'magical' curative powers for a number of diseases of the heart, stomach, blood and nerves. Unfortunately, it has never lived up to the claims. It is of no real help to slimmers as it contains 400 kilojoules in 30 grams (that's about a tablespoonful). Eat enough honey and it may cause tooth decay. It is, however, a natural sweetener with distinctive flavours, which vary according to the source of the nectar selected by the bees. Australian honey is a prized export—about forty per cent of the honey produced in this country finds it way overseas. Honey made from the nectar of a certain species of the eucalypt is a favourite. White clover, blackberry, lucerne and even Salvation Jane or Patterson's Curse are also responsible for honeys with a distinctive flavour.

LEMON TONIC

Put six eggs in a basin and crack their shells. Squeeze the juice of 12 lemons over the eggs and leave for a week. Add one pound of honey and one shilling's worth of rum. Beat the mixture several times daily and bottle. Take one tablespoon daily.

HONEY PORK SPARERIBS

Honey Pork Spareribs:
1.75 kg pork spareribs
½ cup honey
½ cup tomato paste
½ cup beer
½ cup peanut oil
¼ cup worcestershire sauce
2 tablespoons fresh ginger, shredded
2 tablespoons fresh chillies, chopped
3 cloves garlic, crushed
1 teaspoon mustard powder

1 Make a marinade with the honey, tomato paste, beer, peanut oil, worcestershire, ginger, chillies, garlic and mustard powder.
2 Score the skin of the pork spareribs and place them in a large earthenware bowl.
3 Pour the marinade over them, mix well, cover and refrigerate for one to two days.
4 Place the spareribs on a rack in a large baking dish, brush with the marinade and bake at 150°C for one and a half hours, turning the spareribs occasionally.
5 Continue basting the ribs with the marinade during cooking.
6 After one and a half hours, increase the temperature to 200°C and bake for a further 30 minutes.
7 Serve the spareribs with the hot marinade, honeyed sweet potatoes and a salad.

Serves six

HONEYED SWEET POTATOES

Honeyed Sweet Potatoes:
1.5 kg sweet potatoes
salt
60 g butter
⅓ cup honey
grated zest of orange
juice of one orange

1 Place sweet potatoes in a saucepan of boiling salted water and cook until just tender.
2 Drain, peel and slice sweet potatoes lengthways and place in a shallow baking dish.
3 Melt the butter and combine it with the honey, grated zest and orange juice and pour over the sweet potatoes.
4 Place dish in preheated 200°C oven for 20 minutes.

Serves six

HONEY GLAZED CARROTS

Honey Glazed Carrots:
500 g carrots
1 cup chicken stock
60 g butter
¼ cup honey
1 tablespoon finely chopped mint, parsley or coriander

1 Place the carrots, which have been peeled and cut into six cm pieces, or left whole if small, into a large heavy based saucepan together with the stock, butter and honey.
2 Simmer, covered, for 25 minutes.
3 Remove lid and boil mixture rapidly to caramelise the sauce.
4 Add the finely chopped mint, parsley or coriander and serve.

Serves four to six

HONEY SESAME CHICKEN WINGS

1 Place chicken wings in a large earthenware bowl.
2 Combine the honey with the soy sauce, lime or lemon juice, five spice powder and sesame oil.
3 Pour this mixture over the chicken wings, cover and refrigerate for one or two days.
4 Place the wings on a rack in a large baking dish and pour the marinade over them.
5 Bake at 200°C for 15 minutes, then reduce the heat to 150°C and continue cooking and basting for a further 45 minutes.
6 Increase the temperature to 200°C and bake for a further 15 minutes.
7 Remove the wings from the oven and toss them in the sesame seeds.
8 Serve with the hot marinade juices, white rice and a salad.

Honey Sesame Chicken Wings:

1.5 kg chicken wings
1 cup honey
½ cup soy sauce
½ cup fresh lime juice or lemon juice
1 teaspoon five spice powder
1 teaspoon sesame oil
1 cup toasted sesame seeds

NATURAL HONEY ICE CREAM

1 Place the honey in a heavy based saucepan and boil for three minutes to caramelise.
2 Remove from heat and allow bubbles to subside.
3 Beat the eggs until they are light and frothy, then slowly pour in the caramelised honey in a continual stream while continuing to beat the eggs.
4 Continue to beat the mixture for a further five minutes, then refrigerate for 30 minutes.
5 Fold in the whipped cream and pour this mixture into a chilled metal container, then freeze for at least six hours before serving.

Yields two litres

Natural Honey Ice Cream:

½ cup honey
4 large eggs
600 ml cream, whipped

CHILLED HONEYSUCKLE TEA

1 Pour the tea, honey and cloves into a large jug.
2 Stir until the honey is dissolved and allow to cool.
3 Refrigerate until completely chilled.
4 Just before serving, add the cider.
5 Pour into individual chilled glasses and garnish with the thinly sliced orange and the mint.

Serves six

Honeysuckle Tea:

4 cups freshly brewed tea
⅓ cup honey
4 whole cloves
3 cups apple cider, chilled
1 orange, sliced very thinly
sprigs of mint, or fresh apple mint if available

HONEY AND APPLE CONSERVE

Honey & Apple Conserve:

2 cups honey
2 cups cider vinegar
2 teaspoons cloves, finely ground
2 teaspoons cinnamon, finely ground
1 kg peeled, cored and quartered cooking apples

1 Place honey, vinegar, cloves and cinnamon in a heavy based saucepan.
2 Stir over medium heat until dissolved.
3 Add prepared apples and bring to the boil, stirring occasionally.
4 Cook gently and continue to stir until the mixture is thick and smooth. This will take about 45 minutes.
5 Pour into warm sterilised jars and immediately seal and label.

This conserve is excellent with hot or cold ham, pork, duckling or game.

The recipe yields approximately six cups.

Sugar Free

Question I need jam recipes which use no sugar.

Answer The Nutrition Departments of many large hospitals will provide information for those people who need to sustain a sugar-free diet. Often they provide recipe leaflets for a wide variety of sugar-free dishes. The following are examples of jams which do not include sugar.

APRICOT JAM

Apricot Jam:

125 g dried apricots
1 cup orange juice
125 g dried apples
3 cups water
1 tablespoon lemon juice
⅓ cup boiling water
3 teaspoons diabetic lemon jelly crystals
liquid artificial sweetener (optional)

1 Soak the apricots in the orange juice and the apples in water, overnight.
2 Combine the apricots, apples, their liquid and the lemon juice in a large saucepan.
3 Simmer, uncovered, for about one and a half hours.
4 Pulp the fruit.
5 Dissolve the jelly crystals in the boiling water and stir the jelly into the jam.
6 Sweeten to taste.
7 Bottle and seal while still hot.

These jams will keep in the refrigerator for about three weeks. They have no sugar to act as a preservative.

MARMALADE

1 Slice three oranges very finely.
2 Boil for 20 minutes in their own juice.
3 Add one tablespoon of diabetic orange jelly crystals and one teaspoon of Kool C.
4 Bottle while still hot.

STRAWBERRY AND APPLE SPREAD

1 Simmer, for 30 minutes, the strawberries, pie apple, orange and lemon juice in a large pan, stirring frequently.
2 Dissolve the jelly crystals in the hot water.
3 Remove the fruit mixture from the heat and stir in the jelly.
4 Sweeten to taste.
5 Bottle and seal while still hot.

Strawberry & Apple Spread:

500 g fresh strawberries
1½ cups unsweetened pie apple
2 tablespoons lemon juice
2 tablespoons orange juice
⅔ cup hot water
1½ tablespoons strawberry diabetic jelly crystals
artificial liquid sweetener (optional)

Eggless Recipes

Question I have a child with an allergy and I need egg substitutes in recipes. I've heard that vinegar may be used but I don't know how much to use.
Answer The following recipe uses vinegar in place of eggs.

EGGLESS FRUIT CAKE

1 Sift flour, nutmeg, spice and cinnamon three times then rub in butter.
2 Mix in sugar, fruit and peel.
3 Dissolve bicarb soda in milk.
4 Add vinegar and stir quickly into dry mixture. Mix well.
5 Fold in the mashed pumpkin.
6 Place mixture in a prepared 20 cm or eight inch square or round cake tin.
7 Bake in a moderate oven for approximately one and three-quarter hours.
8 Allow to stand in tin about 15 minutes before turning carefully on to a cake cooler. Do not cut until next day.

Eggless Fruit Cake:

450 g plain flour
¼ teaspoon nutmeg
2 teaspoons mixed spice
½ teaspoon cinnamon
170 g butter
170 g sugar
230 g sultanas
230 g currants
115 g chopped cherries
115 g chopped mixed peel
2 teaspoons bicarb soda
140 ml milk
3 tablespoons vinegar
1½ cups dry cooked mashed pumpkin

Citrus Loaf:

3 cups SR flour
grated rind of ½ large orange
¾ cup shredded peel
3 tablespoons golden syrup
60 g butter
1 cup warm milk
pinch of salt

CITRUS LOAF

1 Sift flour and salt.
2 Add orange rind and peel.
3 Melt butter in milk and then dissolve golden syrup in milk.
4 Add milk/butter/golden syrup to dry ingredients and mix to a dough.
5 Turn into a greased loaf-tin.
6 Bake in a moderate (180°C) oven, 55 to 60 minutes.
7 Slice and butter when cool and serve as freshly made as possible.

EGGLESS CAKE ONE

Eggless Cake One:

200 g plain flour
100 g margarine
100 g sugar
30 g cocoa
small cup of milk
½ tablespoon bicarb soda
1 tablespoon malt vinegar

1 Rub the margarine into the flour.
2 Add sugar and cocoa and mix.
3 Warm the milk.
4 Dissolve bicarb in vinegar.
5 Mix together the milk and bicarb/vinegar.
6 Add to flour/margarine mixture.
7 Pour into sandwich tins.
8 Bake in a moderate (180°C) oven for approximately 25 minutes.

EGGLESS CAKE TWO

Eggless Cake Two:

230 g self raising flour
115 g sugar
½ teaspoon bicarb soda
60 g chopped peel
½ teaspoon mixed spice
115 g dried fruit
140 ml milk
1 tablespoon malt vinegar
60 g margarine

1 Sift the flour and spice and rub in the margarine.
2 Add sugar, peel and fruit.
3 Put the bicarb in a basin, mix with the milk and add the vinegar and pour all at once into the dry ingredients.
4 Mix quickly and put into a prepared shallow square tin.
5 Bake in a moderate (180°C) oven for about 35 minutes, until well risen and firm to the touch.
6 Cut into squares when cool.

If using a cake mix, sour milk is a good substitute for egg. Sour the milk naturally, by leaving it in the kitchen in a cup for a day. Two half egg shells of soured milk equals one egg. The soured milk gives a lovely moist cake.

EGGLESS TEA CAKE

1 Mix tea, sugar and currants together.
2 Leave to stand overnight.
3 Add flour and mixed spice and mix well but **do not beat**.
4 Bake mixture in a moderate (180°C) oven for about one hour.
5 When cool, slice and butter.

Eggless Tea Cake:

1 cup strong tea
1 cup currants
1 cup sugar
2 cups self raising flour
1 tsp mixed spice

PEACH CARAMEL CRUNCH

1 Combine flour, oats, sugar, cinnamon and salt.
2 Add butter and mix lightly.
3 Reserve a good half cup of the mixture and press rest into a 23 cm tart plate.
4 Arrange peach slices on top.
5 Sprinkle remaining crumbly mixture over the top of the sliced peaches.
6 Bake half an hour in a moderate (180°C) oven.

Peach Caramel Crunch:

½ cup plain flour
1½ cups quick-cooking rolled oats
⅔ cup brown sugar
1 tsp cinnamon
½ teaspoon salt
½ cup melted butter
sliced peaches

DATE ROLL

1 Place dates, sugar, milk and butter into a saucepan and simmer for ten minutes.
2 When cool, add spice, cinnamon, salt, bicarb soda, vinegar and sifted flour.
3 Mix lightly.
4 Fill two greased nut-roll tins.
5 Bake in a moderate (180°C) oven for 45 minutes.

Date Roll:

1 cup chopped dates
½ cup sugar
1¼ cups milk
60 g butter
½ teaspoon spice
½ teaspoon cinnamon
2 tsps bicarb soda
2 tablespoons vinegar
2½ cups SR flour
pinch of salt

CUT AND COME AGAIN CAKE

1 Mix dry ingredients.
2 Rub in butter and mix to soft dough with the milk ... sour, skim or new.
3 Beat well until bubbles appear.
4 Add vinegar.
5 Pour into prepared tin and bake in a moderate (180°C) oven for about one and a half hours.
6 Leave 24 hours before cutting.

Cut & Come Again Cake:

340 g flour
¾ tsp bicarb soda
2 tsps vinegar
340 g mixed fruit
pinch nutmeg
115 g butter
115 g sugar
a little milk

Chocolate Almond Cake:
2 tablespoons butter
3 tablespoons sugar
½ tsp vanilla
1 tablespoon golden syrup
3 dessertspoons cocoa
½ tsp bicarb soda
1¼ cups flour
2½ tsps baking powder
¼ tsp salt
¾ cup milk
1 dessertspoon coffee essence
warm icing
toasted coconut
almonds

EGGLESS CHOCOLATE ALMOND CAKE

1 Cream butter with sugar, vanilla, and syrup.
2 Add cocoa, blended smoothly with a little milk.
3 Add the coffee essence.
4 Fold in sifted dry ingredients alternately with the balance of the milk.
5 Bake in a 20 cm cake tin in a moderate (180°C) oven for 40 to 50 minutes.
6 Cover with warm icing when cold.
7 Decorate sides with toasted coconut.
8 Decorate top with whole blanched almonds and chocolate icing.

Chocolate Sandwich Cake:
200 g flour
85 g butter
85 g sugar
30 g cocoa
1 tablespoon malt vinegar
½ tsp bicarb soda
small cup of milk

CHOCOLATE SANDWICH CAKE

1 Rub butter into flour.
2 Add sugar and cocoa.
3 Warm the milk and add to the mixture.
4 Dissolve the bicarb in vinegar and mix all together.
5 Place in sandwich tins.
6 Bake 25 minutes in a moderate oven.

Chocolate Sponge:
1½ large cups SR flour
¾ large cup sugar
1 large cup sour milk
1 tsp bicarb soda
2 tablespoons melted butter
½ tsp salt
2 tablespoons cocoa
½ tsp vanilla

CHOCOLATE SPONGE

1 Melt butter.
2 Beat in sugar.
3 Add cocoa and sour milk.
4 Add rest of ingredients and mix well.
5 Bake in two sandwich tins in a hot (205°C) oven for 15 to 20 minutes.

SULTANA LOAF

1 Place into saucepan the milk, bicarb and butter.
2 Bring to boil.
3 Add vinegar.
4 Stir liquid into mixed dry ingredients.
5 Pour into loaf tin.
6 Mix topping ingredients and sprinkle over top of mixture.
7 Bake in moderate (180°C) oven for 30 to 40 minutes.

Sultana Loaf:

2 cups SR flour
1 cup sugar
½ teaspoon cinnamon
½ teaspoon nutmeg
1 cup sultanas
1½ cups milk
1 small teaspoon bicarb soda
1 tablespoon butter
1 teaspoon vinegar
Topping:
1 dessertspoon sugar
1 dessertspoon cinnamon

SPONGE PARKIN OR GINGER CAKE

1 Rub butter into flour.
2 Add dry ingredients and mix well.
3 Stir in golden syrup.
4 Add milk and stir to a dropping consistency.
5 Bake in a moderate (180°C) oven for 30 minutes.

Sponge Parkin/Ginger Cake:

170 g flour
2 tablespoons golden syrup
60 g butter
½ teaspoon bicarb soda
30 g sugar
1 teaspoon ground ginger
pinch salt
milk to mix

OVERNIGHT CAKE

1 Rub butter into flour.
2 Add other dry ingredients.
3 Mix in the milk.
4 Allow to stand overnight.
5 Mix again and bake in a very slow (120°C) oven for approximately one and a half hours.

Overnight Cake:

230 g plain flour
85 g sugar
115 g sultanas
60 g butter
115 g raisins
1 teaspoon nutmeg
60 g peel
½ teaspoon mixed spice
1 teacup milk
1 teaspoon bicarb soda
½ teaspoon salt

It's Impossible

Question Is there a dish called the Impossible Pie? Apparently one throws a whole lot of ingredients in a dish and they sort themselves out.

Answer There is a dish called The Impossible Pie (or Quiche). It has been tested in the *Q&A* Kitchen—and it does work!

IMPOSSIBLE PIE

Impossible Pie:

4 eggs
60 g butter (softened not melted)
½ cup SR flour
2 cups milk
1 cup sugar
1 cup coconut
1 teaspoon vanilla essence
¼ teaspoon salt

1 Put all the ingredients into a blender and blend for 20 seconds.
2 Pour mixture into a greased 25 cm Pyrex dish.
3 Bake at 180°C for an hour or until the centre is firm.

The flour settles to form a crust—the coconut forms a topping—the rest, an egg custard filling.

IMPOSSIBLE QUICHE

Impossible Quiche:

3 eggs
½ cup SR flour
salt and pepper
1 cup milk (or ½ milk ½ cream)
60 g melted shortening

1 Mix all the ingredients together with a fork.
2 Pour into a greased pie dish.
3 Add any of the following (being 'impossible', any addition is possible, within reason): chopped bacon and onion; celery, apple, walnuts and mayonnaise; mushrooms, tomato and onion; corn, asparagus, salami, salmon, parsley, etc, etc.
4 Top with two cups of grated cheese.
5 Bake in a moderate (180°C) oven for one hour or until firm.

QUICK SALMON QUICHE

Quick Salmon Quiche:

6 crushed SAO biscuits
3 eggs
1 small finely grated onion
200 g tin salmon
1 cup milk
salt and pepper
120 g grated cheese

1 Mix all ingredients together and press into a pie plate.
2 Bake at 180°C for about 45 minutes. (Or 20 minutes on simmer in the microwave.)

Chicken Loaf

Question A friend of mine—well, ex-friend really—makes a pressed chicken which is terrific. She won't give me the recipe. Is someone else willing to do so?

Answer A number of listeners were more than willing to part with their recipe for chicken loaf or pressed chicken.

Chicken Loaf:
1 boiling chicken
1 small onion
1 bay leaf
1½ cups evaporated milk
4½ tablespoons butter
3 tablespoons gelatine
1 thick slice of lemon
a few peppercorns and parsley stalks
¼ teaspoon ground thyme
⅔ cup plain flour

1 Line a large loaf tin with foil and grease well.
2 Put chicken into a pan with the onion, lemon, peppercorns, parsley, bay leaf and thyme.
3 Add water to cover, but do **not** add salt.
4 Bring to the boil slowly and cook gently for about one and a half hours, or until tender when tested.
5 Leave until cold and spoon solidified fat from the top of the stock.
6 Lift out chicken. Discard skin and bones and slice flesh thickly. Reheat stock.
7 Strain and measure out three cups.
8 Dissolve gelatine in three quarters of a cup of the stock and mix the remainder with the evaporated milk.
9 Melt the butter and stir in the flour. Cook for two minutes, stirring. Do not let it brown.
10 Gradually stir in the milk stock.
11 Bring to the boil and cook gently for three minutes. Add salt and pepper to taste.
12 Stir in the dissolved gelatine and put the sauce aside until it is lukewarm.
13 Spoon a little of this sauce into the loaf tin, add a layer of sliced chicken, then repeat the layers until all the sauce and chicken are used, ending with a layer of the sauce.
14 Press down firmly and chill well, preferably overnight.
15 Turn out and slice to serve.

Faggots, Ffagodau or Savoury Ducks

Question I've heard of a dish with the intriguing name of faggots. I've never eaten it, but I would like to know what it is and how it is made.

Answer Certain questions on *Q&A* generate an extraordinary amount of interest. This was one. Our mail indicated a lot of people knew what faggots were— despite the fact that most dictionaries list at least four separate meanings for the word! Faggots may be: a bundle of sticks or twigs; a box formed by four pieces of wrought iron; a bouquet garni; or a ball of chopped meat, usually pork liver, bound with herbs and bread and eaten fried.

It was this last our questioner meant when the subject was raised during *Q&A*.

There seem to be as many variations to the recipe as there are listeners to *Q&A*. Traditionally, a pig's caul is used to make faggots, but this is difficult to obtain in Australia. More on the caul later. We give two variations of the recipe—one using the caul and the other not.

WELSH FAGGOTS AND PEAS

Welsh Faggots & Peas:

3 kg lambs fry or calves liver

6 cups soft breadcrumbs

250 g suet, finely sliced

6 large onions, chopped

1 tablespoon fresh sage

salt and pepper to taste

1 Wash the lambs fry or calves liver.
2 Put it through a mincer.
3 Add the remaining ingredients and mix well.
4 Spoon this mixture into a large baking dish and smooth the top.
5 Mark the surface into 5 cm squares with a knife, but do not cut all the way through.
6 Cover with foil and bake in a moderate (180°C) oven for 30 minutes.
7 Remove the foil and bake for a further ten minutes to brown the top.
8 Cut into squares along the lines.
9 Serve hot with cooked dried peas (see p 140), or pease pudding, chunks of bread, and vinegar to sprinkle over the top.

Dried peas are an essential part of this dish. They will be found in the supermarket or corner store. Soak them overnight, drain and cook in boiling salted water until soft. Traditionally, faggots are formed into individual balls, each wrapped in a pig's caul, the membrane which covers the lower part of the pig's intestine. It could be described as one of the earliest forms of sausage skin. The caul is sometimes called the leaf because that is what it resembles, veins of fat connected to each other by a superfine, almost transparent, skin. The caul is also a portion of the amniotic sac, sometimes covering the head of a child at birth. There is a superstitition connected with the caul to the effect that a person born with a caul will never drown. The superstitition was so strong, and may still be, that sailors would buy a caul to protect themselves from drowning at sea.

Here is the traditional method of making faggots with the original imperial measures.

TRADITIONAL METHOD

1 Soak the pig's caul in tepid water.
2 Peel and slice the onions and place them, together with the pig's liver, in a pan and cover with water.
3 Bring to the boil and simmer for 45 minutes.
4 Drain off the liquid.
5 Pour a little, enough to soak, over the breadcrumbs.
6 Mince the pig's liver and onions.
7 Add them to the soaked breadcrumbs.
8 Season with salt and pepper.
9 Beat with a fork until smooth.
10 Cut the caul into two inch squares.
11 Place two tblspns of mixture on each.
12 Shape into balls using the caul as a skin.
13 Pack closely in a roasting pan and bake in a hot (200°C) oven until well browned.

Traditional Method:

1 pig's caul

1 lb pig's liver

3 small onions

3 oz soft white breadcrumbs

½ teaspoon salt

¼ teaspoon pepper

Pepper Pot

Question A couple of weeks ago I ordered a wonderful dish at a local restaurant but I didn't ask for the recipe. The dish was called Pepper Pot and it contained both crab and lamb in a souffle. I'd like the recipe.

Answer Pepper Pot is a very old dish with an appropriate name—the ingredients include cayenne, black pepper, worcestershire sauce, paprika, ground cloves and mustard.

Crab & Lamb Souffle:

185 g crab meat
200 g cooked lamb pieces
1 tablespoon butter
½ cup finely chopped fresh dill
½ cup finely chopped spring onion
¾ cup milk
1 tablespoon cornflour
½ teaspoon salt
½ teaspoon dry mustard
½ teaspoon paprika
¼ teaspoon black pepper
pinch cayenne pepper
pinch ground cloves
pinch cream of tartar
3 eggs, separated
2 teaspoons worcestershire sauce

CRAB AND LAMB SOUFFLE

1 Lightly grease a souffle dish and coat with dry breadcrumbs.
2 Preheat oven to hot (205°C).
3 Flake crab and discard any shell or membrane.
4 Melt butter in a small saucepan.
5 Cook spring onions on low heat till soft and golden.
6 Add dill and cook for one minute longer.
7 Mix cornflour to a smooth paste with a little of the milk.
8 Add remaining milk to saucepan and heat gently.
9 Add all the seasonings to the cornflour and stir into milk in pan. Keep stirring constantly until it thickens.
10 Remove from heat and stir in beaten egg yolks, crab and lamb pieces.
11 Beat egg whites until stiff, adding a pinch of cream of tartar. Gently fold into the crab and lamb mixture. Do not overmix.
12 Pour into souffle dish, place on oven tray and bake for ten minutes then reduce heat to moderate and cook for a further 20 minutes until golden brown and well risen.

Honey Beef and Beans

Question Using honey in a beef dish may seem strange but I have eaten it. Now I'd like to try preparing the dish myself. It also includes canned beans. Can someone help with the recipe?

Answer The following recipe may be the right one

1 Heat oil and butter.
2 Fry onion lightly and remove from pan.
3 Toss meat in seasoned flour.
4 Add to pan (use extra butter if necessary) and fry until well browned, about ten minutes.
5 Add stock, honey, soy sauce, vinegar, tomato sauce.
6 Simmer until meat is tender, about 30 minutes.
7 Ten minutes before serving, fold in the lima beans, parsley and ginger.
8 Serve with boiled rice. Enough for eight.

BALINESE BEEF

Question The request for the recipe for Honey Beef and Beans reminded me of a dish I had once—Balinese Beef, I think it was called. Does anyone have the recipe?

Answer Naturally someone did!

1 Place the first four ingredients in a blender and blend until smooth.
2 Fry this mixture in hot oil.
3 Add meat and stir fry for two minutes.
4 Combine the remaining ingredients.
5 Add to pan and simmer until meat is tender, about ten minutes.
6 Remove the meat pieces and thread onto skewers.
7 Continue simmering the sauce until it is reduced and a little thickened.
8 Brush the meat with the sauce and reheat under grill.
9 Serve with boiled rice.

Coconut Milk: Soak 1 cup of desiccated coconut in 1¼ cups of water for 15 minutes. Drain and squeeze all the liquid from the coconut.

Honey Beef and Beans:

3 tablespoons oil

2 large onions, sliced finely

1 kg topside steak, cut in big strips

4 tablespoons honey

½ cup vinegar

2 × 440 g cans of lima beans (use liquid in stock)

1 level tablespoon finely grated green ginger

3 level tablespoons butter

4 level tablespoons seasoned flour

2 cups beef stock

2 tablespoons soy sauce

1 cup tomato sauce

4 level tablespoons chopped parsley

Balinese Beef:

4 tablespoons soy sauce

4 tablespoons lemon juice

2 onions, chopped roughly

1 tspn black pepper

2 tablespoons oil

1 kg topside, sliced

1 cup coconut milk

3 tspns curry powder

4 lemon peel strips, 5 cm long

1 level tablespoon sugar

Balinese Beef

Gammon

Question Are gammon steaks available in
Australia? If not, is it possible to prepare them at
home?

Answer Gammon is the hind leg of a pig which
has been cured in brine for up to four days and
then matured in a cool, dark room for at least
another ten or eleven days. Gammon is cured as a
complete joint. It is then cut into steaks or smaller
joints as required. After curing gammon may be
smoked or left as it is. Gammon steaks are available
in Australia at specialist delicatessens.

A note on the use of the saltpetre which is essential
in this recipe: without saltpetre the meat may taste
all right but it will look quite unappetising. The
saltpetre imparts a healthy-looking, rosy colour.

When making gammon the following brine is used:

1 To the water add the salt, sugar and saltpetre.
2 Add the aromatics or spices.
3 Bring the lot to the boil.
4 Skim the liquid.
5 Remove from the heat and allow to cool.
6 Clean a plastic container (large enough to
   contain the leg with room to spare) with boiling
   water and washing soda.
7 Rinse and allow to drain. The rinsing process
   ensures that no moulds are present during the
   curing.
8 Clean a stone and a lid for the container in the
   same way.
9 Strain the brine into the container and
   submerge the meat in it.
10 Weigh down the meat with the stone to ensure
   it is completely covered by brine.
11 Cover the container with the lid to keep out the
   air.
12 Remove gammon from brine after no fewer than
   four days.
13 Dry gammon, hang in a cool, dark place and
   allow to mature for about ten days.

Brine:

3 litres water

300 g sea or rock salt

300 g brown sugar

55 g saltpetre

1 teaspoon juniper berries

3 sprigs thyme

small piece nutmeg

1 teaspoon black peppercorns

1 bay leaf

4 cloves

The brine may be used again, but should be re-boiled, cleaned and fortified every so often. It is not wise to mix meats in the same batch of brine. The brine should be discarded when a white mould begins to appear on the surface. Should this happen while the brine is being used do not worry—the meat will not be affected. Different degrees of curing are reached by varying the soaking time.

Smoked Chicken (Peking Style)

Question I buy smoked chicken from the supermarket. Is it possible to smoke chicken at home?

Answer Yes, but don't get busted.

Smoked Chicken:

1 young ½ kg chicken
1½ tablespoons salt
1 sliced green onion
2 tablespoons brown peppercorns
3 slices ginger
2 slices star anise
1 cm cinnamon stick
1 cup soy sauce
8 cups boiling water
½ cup flour
½ cup black tea leaves
1 tablespoon sesame oil

1 Cook peppercorns and salt in a dry frypan over low heat for about one minute.
2 Clean and wipe chicken and rub with peppercorn/salt mix.
3 Let chicken sit for at least five hours.
4 Add green onion, ginger, star anise, cinnamon and soy sauce to eight cups of boiling water in a large pan.
5 Cook for ten minutes.
6 Add chicken and cook for further ten minutes, turning it once.
7 Remove and cool.
8 Line a heavy lidded pan with aluminium foil to assist cleaning later.
9 Place sugar, flour and tea leaves in pan.
10 Place chicken on its side on a rack in the pan.
11 Cover and cook over low heat for eight minutes.
12 Turn chicken and smoke for five more minutes.
13 Remove chicken from pan and brush with sesame seed oil.
14 When cool, slice into 2.5 cm by 5 cm pieces and arrange in a chicken shape on serving plate.

You might prefer to smoke this chicken out of doors on a primus stove or a barbecue.

Mutton

IRISH STEW

1 Cut the lamb or mutton into cubes.
2 Peel the potatoes and onions and cut them into chunks.
3 Chop the parsley and thyme together.
4 Butter a casserole and arrange a layer of one third of the potatoes on the bottom of the casserole. Cover with a layer of the lamb then a layer of the onions.
5 Season with the herbs, salt and pepper.
6 Repeat the layering process until all the ingredients are used up, ending with a layer of onions, then add the stock.
7 Cover and cook in a 180°C oven for one and a half hours until the lamb or mutton is tender.
8 Combine the butter and flour in a small bowl and stir this paste into the casserole.
9 Continue cooking for five minutes until the juices have thickened.
10 Serve garnished with extra finely chopped parsley.

Irish Stew:

1.5 kg stewing lamb or mutton
6 large potatoes
4 white onions
2 tablespoons finely chopped parsley
1 teaspoon dried thyme
1 teaspoon salt
freshly ground black pepper
1½ cups chicken stock
1½ tablespoons softened butter
1 tablespoon flour

MUTTON CURRY

1 Fry the chops in hot dripping until brown, then remove from the pan.
2 Add the chopped onion, apple and other ingredients, except the flour and stock.
3 Cook until brown.
4 Add the flour and mix well.
5 Add the stock and stir until mixture boils.
6 Return the chops to the pan, cover and cook gently for two hours, until the meat is tender.
7 Serve with mashed potatoes or rice.

Mutton Curry:

1 kg neck chops
1 tablespoon dripping
1 large green apple
1 large onion
1 teaspoon salt
pinch cayenne
1 dessertspoon curry powder (or to taste)
2 cups stock
1 tablespoon chutney
1 tablespoon tomato sauce
1 tablespoon raisins
2 tablespoons flour
1 tablespoon golden syrup
1 tablespoon coconut
1 tablespoon vinegar

AUSTRALIAN GOOSE

Take two or three flaps of mutton (depending on the size of the family) and put in the bottom of a large stewing pan or boiler. Add one onion, one carrot, three cloves, three peppercorns, a sprig of celery, salt and pepper.

Simmer slowly in enough water to just cover the flaps. When quite tender, take out and bone. Press between two dishes and leave until the next day. Save the liquor. When the meat is quite cold and firm, trim nicely; roll in egg and breadcrumbs and grill slowly, until golden brown. Make a sauce from the liquor and flavour it with a little cayenne pepper, lemon and a spoonful of sherry, if available.

Mock Fish

Mr Cullen's mother, who lived to be 100 years of age, had some very original cooking ideas, one of which won the first prize in the 'Breakfast Dish' Competition in the *Country Life and Stock and Station Journal* of Friday, May 2, 1941. Mrs Cullen, who was delighted to 'score and win' bought War Savings Certificates with her prize. The following is an extract from *Country Life*.
MOCK FISH - SELECTED AS BEST BREAKFAST DISH - TASTY AND ECONOMICAL. The judges have selected the entry of Mrs SA Cullen, Laggan, as the best tasty and economic breakfast dish entered in our competition. It is a "mock fish" recipe that deceived the judges when they made it up! The basis of the recipe is parsnips, of which a few are to be found in most country kitchen gardens, and eggs, which are found easily enough on farm and station—when the hens are laying! Mrs Cullen, to whom the guinea prize is being posted, says that even fishermen have been deceived—we can well believe that.

Here is the recipe:

MOCK FISH

Boil some good sized parsnips in salted water until tender, but not broken. Let them cool and then cut lengthwise. If the parsnips are large enough the cuts will resemble fillets of fish. Dip them in batter and fry till brown.

That's all there is to it, now all you have to do is try it yourself.

MOCK TURKEY

1 Soak the rabbit for one hour, changing the water twice, then joint it, wipe dry and roll in seasoned flour.
2 Fry in a little fat until golden brown, then lift into a casserole.
3 Fry chopped vegetables and add them to the casserole.
4 Make a gravy with the fat in the pan and two tablespoons of flour, the meat extract, sauce or tomato, some water, and the vinegar.
5 Pour the boiling sauce over the casserole and cook one and a half to two hours on a low heat.

Mock Turkey:
1 young rabbit
1 carrot
1 onion
1 tablespoon chopped parsley
½ cup finely chopped celery
flour
1 teaspoon meat extract (Bonox or Bovril)
1 tablespoon tomato sauce or 1 chopped tomato
½ cup vinegar, simmered and reduced with 6 crushed allspice berries, then strained

Bubble and Squeak

Question I'm curious about the term 'bubble and squeak'. How did it originate and does someone have a genuine, original recipe?

Answer 'When midst the frying pan, in accents savage, the beef, so surly, quarrels with the cabbage.'

There was considerable discussion among our correspondents as to the correct ingredients for Bubble and Squeak. There was agreement however, that it **must** contain cabbage. The request for information about the dish set mouths a-watering, memories a-bubbling and pens a-squeaking.

The dish gets its name from the sound made while cooking.

MERCUROCHROME STAIN
The stains left by spilt merchurochrome can be removed. Cover them with calamine lotion, allow to dry, then brush off.

STEAM IRONS

Always empty steam irons after use. If water is left in the iron between ironing sessions, sediment build-up can become a problem.

Tom Evans: I go back seventy years to my mother's hotel in Hobart, Tasmania. My aunty did the cooking at the hotel and my father, who came from the USA, insisted she cook his breakfast which consisted partly of Bubble and Squeak. It was also served to the guests and boarders at the hotel. Years later I re-visited Hobart and ran into one of my mother's permanent boarders, who had since married. The first thing he asked me was, 'What was the recipe for your mother's Bubble and Squeak?' He wanted his wife to give him his old-time breakfast. As a lad I asked my father why it was called Bubble and Squeak and he said because it 'bubbles in the pan and squeaks on the plate'.

Thelma Parkinson: When I was a child many years ago, our staple green vegetable was packet green peas, which were soaked overnight in boiling water with a good pinch of bicarbonate of soda. (Modern cooks would throw up their hands in horror!) Next evening the peas were put in a calico bag in which our flour was bought. Then peas and bag were put in boiling salted water and in a matter of minutes the peas were cooked. Should we have a meat pie for dinner and any be left over, next morning at breakfast it was chopped up and put in a heavy frying pan in which rich gravy-based beef dripping was melted. Then all left-overs, vegetables such as boiled mashed potato, cabbage and any meat from the previous dinner, such as mutton or roast beef, were added. **But,** packet green peas are a must in Bubble and Squeak, as well as salt and pepper.

June Trend: Bubble and Squeak ingredients (no relation to fried-up vegetables) can be a very serious matter. I can recall my horror on a trip abroad when informed by a British housewife that Brussels sprouts, not cabbage, must be fried with potatoes, for this dish to be correct. Not cabbage? Heresy! No wonder the British needed outside help to win their wars. I seethed. Off the record, I now cheat a little, by adding a touch of onion to the pan, but other common garden vegetables—never!

Greg Beech: I think that the concoction known colloquially as Bubble and Squeak comes from a strange mixture that used to be served as 'late supper' during my time in the RAF in World War II. The ingredients were a mystery really to anyone unfortunate enough to confront it. I think that the main ingredient was cabbage, as it had the characteristic pong of boiling cabbage. If you could put up with the effluvium, though, it was quite tasty. The song, 'Ah, sweet mystery of life at last I've found you' was no doubt its signature tune. If you heard strains of this tune filtering through the light mist of evening you would, as a rule, turn about and go to bed hungry, or grab some slices of bread and make toast in front of the billet stove.

BALLPOINTS AND LEATHER

Ballpoint ink and leather do not always go together. The ink may be removed from the leather with eucalyptus oil.

BUBBLE AND SQUEAK

An Early Victorian Recipe

This useful old-fashioned dish is made of cold boiled beef. If the beef has been salted, it will be more tasty. Cut the meat into thin slices with a very little fat and fry it very lightly in butter. Have ready a good sized savoy cabbage boiled without the outside leaves. Shred it very small. Add pepper and salt to taste. Put it into the frying pan as soon as the meat is taken out, which must be kept hot before the fire. It will take more butter to fry the cabbage, which must be well shaken about till thoroughly done; then spread over a dish and the slices of meat laid upon it. Garnish the dish with pickled cucumbers and walnuts.

MRS BEETON'S BUBBLE AND SQUEAK

Method: Melt a little butter or fat in a frying pan, put in meat, fry quickly until lightly browned on both sides, then remove and keep hot. Put in the onion, fry until brown, add the potatoes and greens and season to taste. Stir until thoroughly hot, then add a little vinegar, if liked, and turn onto a hot dish. Place the slices of meat on the top and serve.

Time—about 20 minutes.

Mrs Beeton's Recipe:

thin slices of cold roast or boiled beef

cold mashed potatoes

cold greens of any kind

1 onion shredded

butter or dripping

salt and pepper

vinegar

MRS ROWLEY'S BUBBLE AND SQUEAK

Mash four potatoes and chop a handful of cold cooked greens with a saltspoon of salt and the same of pepper. Mix well together and fry in three ounces of butter, stirring all the time. Keep hot. Cut some thin slices of cold beef into neat slices. Fry slightly over low heat for about six minutes. Put the vegetables around the dish and the meat in the centre, or pile the vegetables in a high cone in the centre of a serving dish, with the slices of meat around. Serve very hot!

IRISH BUBBLE AND SQUEAK
Colcannon

Mix equal parts of cold, chopped boiled cabbage and cold, boiled mashed potatoes. Cook in hot fat and season with salt and pepper. Serve very hot. A little chopped onion is sometimes added. If you wish to be really grand, dice some lean bacon and add that also.

Early Settler's and Johnny Cakes

Early Settler's Cake:

2 cups dripping
2 cups sugar
one emu egg
melon seeds
2 teaspoons bicarb of soda
4 teaspoons cream of tartar
6 cups flour
2 cups goats milk
2 cups currants (optional)

EARLY SETTLER'S CAKE

Cream dripping and sugar. Add emu egg and beat well. Flavour with broken up melon seeds. Sift bicarbonate of soda and cream of tartar with flour. Add goat's milk. You can also add two cups of currants. Bake in a moderate oven in three large tins.

from the 'Como Cookery Book', reprinted by courtesy of The National Trust of Australia

JOHNNY CAKES

1 Sift flour and baking powder.
2 Cream sugar and butter.
3 Add eggs, then the dry ingredients, and milk.
4 Bake in greased patty pans in a moderate oven.

Johnny Cakes:
1 cup corn meal
2 cups flour
1 cup milk
2 oz lard or butter
1 oz sugar
3 eggs
3 tablespoons baking powder

Pastrami

Question I've been told it's difficult to make pastrami at home, but I'd like to try. Could someone provide the recipe?

Answer It takes about a week to make pastrami at home, but the result is well worth the waiting.

1 Rinse brisket or silverside and wipe dry.
2 Combine garlic with pickling spice, paprika, chilli powder, allspice and brown sugar and mix to a thick, coarse paste.
3 Rub meat all over with mixture and wrap closely in plastic food wrap.
4 Place in a sealed container and store in the refrigerator from four days up to a week. Turn the meat occasionally, still in its wrap.
5 To cook, unwrap meat and place in a deep pan, just large enough to contain it, adding any liquid from the meat.
6 Cover with warm water and add the onion, parsley, bacon bones and vinegar. Bring to a slow simmer, cover and simmer gently for two to two and a half hours until tender.
7 Remove from heat and let stand, in liquid, for 15 minutes before serving.

Slice very thin and serve with hot potato salad, steamed cabbage and rye bread.

Return the unsliced meat to the pan to complete cooling in the liquid. Drain, wrap in plastic food wrap and store in refrigerator. Pastrami can also be served cold.

Pastrami:
2 kg piece rolled corned brisket or silverside
1 teaspoon paprika
3 large cloves garlic, crushed
2 teaspoons pickling spice
¼ teaspoon hot chilli powder
¼ teaspoon ground allspice
2 tablespoons brown sugar
warm water
1 onion, sliced
2 sprigs parsley
500 g smoked bacon bones
1 tablespoon brown vinegar

Black Pudding

Question You may think this is a strange request but I'd like a recipe for black pudding. Most of my friends are very good cooks and during a discussion about food the other night, I rashly said I could make black pudding. Now I feel I must produce a reasonable example.Could someone provide the recipe?

Answer Most recipes for black pudding start with the instruction: 'Take three pints of blood ...' Although the recipes may sound suitable for a vampire banquet, in fact the main ingredient for black pudding is **always** blood.

Black pudding, also known as blood pudding, is one of the earliest sausages ever made. The original casings were horseshoe-shaped membranes and that remains the traditional shape of the black pudding. However, with the increased use of plastic casings, the sausage is now often straight.

Black, or blood, pudding is served in most countries of Europe and in the British Isles. In England and Ireland it is usually accompanied with bacon and potatoes. In France, Italy and Spain, it is more often simmered in a good stock and served with fried beans.

We forwarded the following recipes to our Questioner. Whether or not she ever presented her food-loving friends with a finished product we do not know.

Black Puddings:

1 quart blood
1 quart grits or coarsely ground oatmeal or boiled rice
winter savory
thyme
pennyroyal
pepper and salt
ground spice
3 lbs beef suet or pig fat
6 eggs

BLACK PUDDINGS

The blood must be stirred with salt until cold. Put a quart of it to a quart of grits (or coarsely ground oatmeal) or boiled rice and soak some bread in milk. Clean the grits well with salt and water. Chop winter savory, thyme, pennyroyal, pepper, and salt, and a little ground spice. Mix these about with three pounds of beef suet or the fat of the pig. Add six eggs, well beaten up. Then add the rice, or grits and bread and fill your skins.

White puddings are made in a similar way with cream, without the blood, but are far inferior in taste or goodness.

BOUDINS NOIRS

A plastic funnel should be used when filling the casings. You will also need a chip-basket, or something similar, to immerse the *boudins* in hot water.

1 Soak the breadcrumbs in the cream or evaporated milk.
2 Add the seasonings including the rum to the blood.
3 Cut the pork fat into small cubes.
4 Melt about 220 g in a heavy frypan.
5 Add the chopped onions and cook slowly until translucent but not brown.
6 Add the rest of the pork fat, then the cream and breadcrumb mixture.
7 Add the blood and stir well.
8 Fit the end of the sausage casing over the funnel.
9 Spoon the mixture into the funnel and force it carefully into the casing. Do not fill the casing too full, as the filling swells when cooked.
10 Knot or twist the casing at appropriate lengths.
11 Allow the sausages or puddings to coil in the chip-basket as they are filled and knotted.
12 Make sure you leave enough casing at the end to be knotted.
13 Boil water in a pan large enough to take the chip basket containing the *boudins*.
14 Remove the pan from the heat and allow the water to come off the boil before immersing the chip basket containing the *boudins*. If the water remains on the boil, the sausages will be spoilt.
15 Return the pan to a low heat for about 20 minutes. After about a quarter of an hour, prick the sausages very gently. They are cooked if a brown liquid comes out. If blood oozes, then the sausages need a further five minutes cooking time.
16 Transfer the chip basket carefully into a bowl of cold water and allow to stand for one minute.
17 Remove the boudins from the cold water and lay on a flat surface to cool.

Boudins Noirs:

sausage casings, in a bowl of water
120 g breadcrumbs
800 ml thick cream (evaporated milk may be used)
3 litres of blood
100 g salt
1 teaspoon mixed spices
1 teaspoon brown sugar
chopped parsley, or chives, or sage
1 tot of rum
1.5 kg pork fat
1.5 kg onions, chopped

BLACK PUDDING IN A TIN

Black Pudding in a Tin:

1 lb loaf of bread
4 or 5 onions
2 oz oatmeal
8 oz cooked rice
4 oz cooked barley
1 lb pig's fat
salt and pepper
marjoram
1 pint blood

Soak a one pound loaf of bread in cold water, then squeeze into a bowl. Add four or five onions, two ounces of oatmeal, eight ounces of cooked rice, four ounces of cooked barley, one pound of pig's fat cut into small pieces, salt, pepper and marjoram to taste. Mix well then add one pint of blood and mix again. Turn this mixture into a large baking tin and bake till firm and set, in a moderate (180°C) oven.

This black pudding can be sliced as required and fried with bacon.

SIMPLE BLACK PUDDING

Simple Black Pudding:

1 quart fresh pig's blood
½ pint milk
1 lb threaded suet
onions to taste
1 oz oatmeal (toasted in oven)
salt and pepper to taste
skins made from pig's intestines

1 Let the blood run into a deep dish, stirring all the time.
2 Add a teaspoon of salt, stir again and rub through a very fine sieve.
3 Add milk and mix well.
4 Add the suet, minced onions, oatmeal, salt and pepper.
5 Mix well, then put mixture into the skins without quite filling them.
6 Tie them in equal lengths.
7 Have ready a pot full of boiling water and just before immersing the puddings, throw in a little cold water to reduce the temperature slightly and prevent the puddings from bursting.
8 Cook for five minutes, then prick the puddings with a needle.
9 Cook gently for a further two hours.
10 Remove from water and hang them to dry in a cool place.
11 When required, heat the black puddings in hot water and then broil. Or slice and fry in dripping.

Toad in the Hole

Question What is toad in the hole?

Answer It is a favourite dish for many people and is made from sausages, or other meats, and batter.

1 Sift flours and salt into a mixing bowl.
2 Make a well in the centre.
3 Pour the egg and two tablespoons of the milk/water into the well.
4 Using a wooden spoon, and working from the centre, gradually mix some of the flour from the edges into the egg and milk.
5 Beat well until smooth.
6 Gradually add half the liquid, beating gently and drawing in the rest of the flour until all is mixed and the batter is smooth and bubbly.
7 Stir in remaining liquid.

Standard Batter:
60 g plain flour
60 g self raising flour
pinch salt
1 egg
285 ml milk and water mixed

TOAD ONE

1 Thoroughly grease a baking dish and heat in a hot oven for ten minutes.
2 Place ½ kg of cooked sausages, halved and skinned, in baking dish.
3 Pour in batter.
4 Return to oven (near the top) for about three quarters of an hour.
5 Serve at once.

TOAD TWO

1 Cut ½ kg of good beef steak into 2 cm cubes.
2 Place meat in greased baking dish.
3 Pour in batter, making sure that two or three pieces of the meat have their 'heads' above the surface.
4 Bake in a moderate oven for one and a half hours until the batter is nicely brown.
5 Serve at once.

TOAD THREE

1 Heat a greased baking dish.

2 Place in it four small lamb chops and two halved tomatoes.

3 Cook for ten minutes in a hot oven.

4 Pour in batter to cover.

5 Return to oven.

6 Cook for 20 minutes, then reduce heat slightly for a further ten minutes.

7 Serve at once.

Microwave Tips

MAKE-UP STAINS

Place a cotton wool pad on top of the stain. Dab the underside of the stain with more cotton wool which has been soaked in a safe dry cleaning fluid. Repeat this process until the make-up stain has been transferred to the top pad of cotton wool, then wash in a reliable detergent.

If you have acquired a microwave oven, do not discard prized recipes collected over the years. They can be converted for microwave cooking.

Time: Microwave time is one quarter to one third that of conventional cooking time for recipes requiring High power, and one third to one half for recipes requiring Medium power. These times do **not** apply to dehydrated foods or tough cuts of meat.

Seasoning: Quantities of seasonings should be halved if they are greater than one teaspoon in the conventional recipe. Do not add salt to foods until after they have finished cooking.

Liquids: The amount of liquid should be reduced in microwave cooking. Usually liquids are not evaporated in the microwave. Decrease the amount of liquid in the conventional recipe by about one third. This rule, however, does not apply in the case of reconstituted foods such as potatoes or rice. If the recipe calls for evaporation of liquids, then it is better to use conventional cooking methods.

Fats and oils can be eliminated from most conventional recipes, unless small amounts are needed for flavouring.

The size of the cooking vessel should be increased. Foods prepared in a microwave have a tendency to bubble because of the speed of cooking.

Doubling the ingredients in a microwave recipe will usually increase the cooking time by one half.

Index

CONTRIBUTORS

Listeners who contributed recipes to previous Q & A books (The Q & A Collection Vols I, II and III) were acknowledged in those books. Additional recipes in this book were contributed by:

Chris Varna (Cumquat and Carrot Marmalade), Meredith Kelly (Traditional German Stollen), Margaret Pointer (Auntie's Pudding, Bondi Pudding, Melbourne Pudding, Johnny Cakes, To Roast an Udder [from The Good Housewife 1756]), Loris Wells (Hunter Valley Casserole, Stuffed Nullarbor Lamb, Rabbit Pie), Pat Hoskins (Brownies, Kangaroo Tail Soup, Mutton Curry, Yabbies), Lis Crookes (Sheep's Head Saute, Early Settler's Cake, Kangaroo Steamer, Tips: Cockroaches, Mushrooms, Sunstroke), Mary Moore (Damper), Elizabeth Lidden (Steamed Kangaroo or Wallaby, Australian Goose), Pat Cullen (Mock Fish), Dorothy Palmer (Mock Turkey), Pat Connolly (Traditional Pavlova), Eunice Hogue (Baked Barracouta), Mick Darton (Boxty, Irish Stew), Zena Low (Golden Lemon Puffs), Joan Hyatt (Apple Blossom Pie), Elisa Mul (Mother Eve's Pudding, from A Taste of Australia in Food and Pictures by Peter Taylor, Pan 0 330 27005 2), Jenny Burnham (Rollmops), Joey Roque (Leche Flan).